Our friend, James Goll, has fa years. We have watched him r grow in faith, hope, and love in his arduous journey. May the lessons he has learned grip your heart and inspire you so that you, too, can become a hero of hope in our generation.

Michael W. & Debbie Smith | michaelwsmith.com

Tell Your Heart to Sing Again is raw and real life. It is a true-life story of love and loss and regaining hope through it all. Navigating through such suffering and being willing to share with others is a great gift, and James has done an excellent job. Thank you, James, for your transparency and for writing this book.

Bill & Beni Johnson | bjm.org and benij.org

We're so grateful James took the time to pen this portion of his life's story, one filled with lessons learned from the trenches. May many be strengthened and encouraged so they, too, may be ambassadors of hope.

John & Lisa Bevere | messengerinternational.com

The life of our friend, James Goll, is a testimony of God's endless hope. With decades of experience in bringing hope to churches and individuals, James writes from a rich treasury of insight. *Tell Your Heart to Sing Again* is your opportunity to taste and see how good God's plan is for your life. Read it for the riches it contains and let hope live again inside of your heart!

Lance Wallnau | www.7mu.com

Life can have many twists and turns. It's not how you start the race but how you finish. As you read this book, listen with your heart so you, too, can emerge from any fiery trials better than when you went in.

Brian & Candice Simmons | thepassiontranslation.com

Hard times will come to everyone, but few make it through complexities with strength still in their step. Through real-life tales of resilience and key biblical insights, James Goll lights a beacon of hope that shines brightly with the testimony of Jesus Christ. Read and be encouraged— and just watch as that encouragement spreads to others!

Dr. Ché & Sue Ahn | cheahn.org

Do you need perspective on the trails of life and tools to help you to keep moving forward? I know this man and his life. The wisdom contained in this book will give you hope and be a source of good news to you.

Cindy Jacobs | generals.org

In *Tell Your Heart to Sing Again*, you will journey with James Goll as he uses his words to surgically open his own heart to share with you the treasures of life he has gained. This is an essential legacy gift from a true father of the faith.

Mickey Robinson | mickeyrobinson.com

In *Tell Your Heart to Sing Again*, James intentionally pushes past the boundaries of safe subjects and pat answers and reminds us that hope is both a disposition and a helmet. This book may be coming into your hands at the very moment you need to secure your helmet. You can trust James. I do.

Harry R. Jackson Jr. | thehopeconnection.org

James identifies heroes in his own walk through tremendous tragedy. However, I found myself thinking, *James Goll is my hero*. This book will provide you with the necessary guardrails for finding and staying connected to the goodness of God and a lifeline of hope.

Johnny & Elizabeth Enlow | johnnyandelizabeth.com

Tell Your Heart to Sing Again shines a light through the darkness for those struggling through situations of loss, pain, confusion, and illness. James combines practical wisdom with his own moments of revelation as he passed through the valley of the shadow of death to produce the reality of overcoming faith. If you apply the lessons James learned, I believe you, too, will be numbered among those who overcame by the blood of the lamb and the word of their testimony.

Joan Hunter | joanhunter.org

Your destiny can be born in life's darkest moments. I know. Like James, my life went into a downward spiral until I discovered the God of hope. This book will feed your soul, and you'll find hope right in front of you.

Danny Gokey | *American Idol* finalist,
author of *Hope in Front of Me*

Tell Your Heart to Sing Again may be the most important book James Goll has ever written. James is one of the most unique leaders I know. His soul is a deep well. He is a theologian and a man of the Spirit. You will definitely discover hope for your life. Get ready to be strengthened and encouraged in the ways of God.

Brian "Head" Welch | recording artist, author

Do you need hope? Do you need strength? Do you need a song in your heart as you walk through to victory? I have watched James walk through some of the most horrific challenges that one can endure. He knows how to take God's hand through the valley of the shadow of death and come through with hope as his greatest weapon. This book is for you!

Patricia King | author, minister, television host, patriciaking.com

Jesus said that we are to keep our hands to the plow and keep looking straight ahead. Over the last few years, we have observed this type of lifestyle in our friend James Goll, which gives him the authority to speak on this topic. If you need some lessons in hope and to how rebuild your life, then *Tell Your Heart to Sing Again* was composed with you in mind.

Henry & Alex Seeley | co-pastors of The Belonging Co., Nashville, TN

Paul tells us in Romans 5 that the road to character involves suffering, but it seems like we are never prepared for the type suffering that comes our way. Everyone can connect to *Tell Your Heart to Sing Again* and be challenged to respond to the Lord in the way that James Goll has responded. His vulnerability and honesty are both refreshing and helpful!

Dr. Don Finto | founder of the Caleb Company, author, and international speaker, Nashville, TN

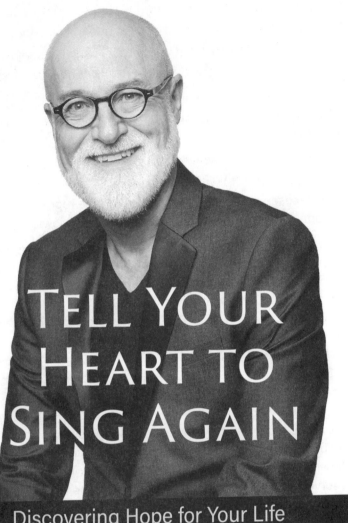

TELL YOUR HEART TO SING AGAIN

Discovering Hope for Your Life

JAMES W. GOLL

Foreword by KRIS VALLOTTON

BroadStreet
PUBLISHING

BroadStreet Publishing Group®, LLC
Savage, Minnesota, USA
www.broadstreetpublishing.com

TELL YOUR HEART TO SING AGAIN: Discovering Hope for Your Life
Copyright © 2020 James W. Goll

978-1-4245-6066-0 (paperback)
978-1-4245-6071-4 (e-book)

Stock or custom editions of BroadStreet Publishing titles may be purchased in bulk for educational, business, ministry, fundraising, or sales promotional use. For information, please email info@broadstreetpublishing.com.

Cover and interior by Garborg Design at GarborgDesign.com

Printed in the United States of America

20 21 22 23 24 5 4 3 2 1

DEDICATION

As you read this raw and transparent book, you will eventually come to the chapter "Never, Never, Never Give Up!" For those of you who know my life, history, and stories, you already know what I am referring to. But I will not spoil the story line of the roller coaster ride contained in this book of redemption and the stunning statement concerning the admonition never to quit. But you will understand in due time.

With this backdrop, I dedicate this book to my late wife, Michal Ann Goll, and to the ministry she founded, Compassion Acts, that we carry on in her honor to the nations to this day. She has been worshipping unabated in heaven now for several years.

Michal Ann, you gave me hope. You never lost your smile. You were the most Christ-like person I ever knew close up. Yes, I am forever a better man because God sent you, my all-American girl, into my life.

We will meet again at the waterside.

Acknowledgments

Years ago, I was taught to pray for three things on a regular basis: to ask God for the release of the fullness of the fruit of the Holy Spirit in order to have character to carry the gifts he gives; to pray for the fullness of the power of the Holy Spirit to release something that lasts beyond simply man's efforts; to pray for the wisdom ways of God in every facet of church and kingdom life.

Perhaps this book you hold in your hands goes more into this third category of prayer for the wisdom ways of God in every facet of life. I never dreamed I'd walk through the valley of the shadow of death. For me, Psalm 23 is a psalm for the living. The book of Psalms has been my guiding light for many years...and the book of Proverbs...and the book of John... and the book of... Well, I'm sure you get the picture.

So I want to give credit where credit is due—to all the writers of the sixty-six very diverse books of the Holy Bible. In doing so, I wish to honor God the Father, the Son, and the Holy Spirit—the Three in One.

The Bible has been my mainstay. My Bible is my close friend. The ultimate Author of this unique Holy Book is the One who gives me life, hope, and resiliency to keep on bouncing back. Thank you, God, for the Bible. Thank you, God, for abounding in hope! Thank you, Papa God, for another opportunity to discover hope for my own personal life and share that with others.

CONTENTS

Foreword by Kris Vallotton

Historically, the church has not always excelled at walking with people through their pain. We know how to rejoice with those who rejoice, yet we often fall short of Christ's standard when it comes to mourning with those who mourn. Our Savior wept with his bereaved friends at the tomb of Lazarus, yet many Christians today are more likely to respond to tragedy with poorly reasoned explanations, weak attempts to cheer, or dark hints that the mourners should have had more faith.

Sadly, I am no exception. In my unconscious ignorance, I used to casually joke about Christians needing antidepressants until depression became profoundly personal. My family went through a terrible crisis that lasted two years. I put all of my time, energy, and thought into helping them, pushing beyond my soul's capacity to cope with such extensive amounts of pain. I started experiencing high levels of anxiety that taxed my mind and body like a plague. Before long, I found myself in a battle with anxiety and depression that left me hopelessly glued to my couch for months. Every day was a living hell as I fell deeply into a seemingly endless pit of despair. At last, I was set free in a moment when I heard God's resounding truth for my situation and chose to believe it. This book you are holding is full of the same kind of shackle-breaking power and illuminating truth.

As you can imagine, my compassion for people walking through anxiety, depression, and grief has grown astronomically since my nervous breakdown, and I've since had the privilege of walking many others through their darkest seasons. I've come to find that when people are grieving, they don't need answers as much as they need empathy. In these pages, you will find both. After walking through terrible loss himself, James Goll understands the process of pain and the purpose of grief as well as the tormenting guilt and questions they can ignite. He also understands that grief is a process, not a place where we set up camp for the remainder of our lives. Mourning is God's way of bringing closure to our pain. In fact, I'd like to propose that true grief leads us not to despair but rather to renewal. Wherever you are on that highway to wholeness, *Tell Your Heart to Sing Again* will help guide you to your destination: new levels of peace, promise, and purpose.

If you've picked up this book, I imagine that you or your family have found yourselves facing a mountain of pain that feels impossible to summit. Grief is not the end of your story! Romans 8:28 tells us "all things work together for good to those who love God" (NKJV). In other words, if it's not good, it's not the end. We have a good God who promises that you will get through this and that the darkness will not consume you. I can tell you from experience that it is possible to emerge from a season of heartache and disappointment healed, hopeful, and wholly free. Mary Anne Radmacher once said, "Courage doesn't always roar. Sometimes courage is the little voice at the end of the day that says *I'll try again tomorrow*."[1]

I pray that God will meet you in these pages and give you

---

1   Mary Anne Radmacher, *Courage Doesn't Always Roar*, 2009, Conari Press

fresh courage for tomorrow, faith for today, and hope for a future glistening with joy and possibility.

Kris Vallotton

Senior Leader, Bethel Church

Co-founder of Bethel School of Supernatural Ministry

Author of thirteen books, including *The Supernatural Ways of Royalty*, *Spirit Wars*, and *Poverty, Riches and Wealth*

Introduction

HAS HARDSHIP EVER STRUCK YOUR HOUSE?

"The Long and Winding Road" was a popular hit song years ago. I loved the haunting melody, but as a disciple in Jesus, I was sure that my path would be smooth and easy. Was I ever wrong! My life has not circled a cul de sac, but it seems to have steered off the primary highway and onto a trail leading to who knows where. It was a road I was unfamiliar with and one that I was not expecting. Twelve or more years were filled with winding roads and an unfair share of trauma along the way. My heart became dead. Well, at least part of it.

As a result, I decided to make lemonade out of lemons as I went on an intentional journey to discover what it would take to revive my own heart and soul. I did not pick this subject. I would never have picked it. If it had been up to me, I would have run a hundred miles in the opposite direction. But in the providence of God, I think this topic has chosen me. I now realize that God has called me to be an ambassador of hope and to call others into this resilient, bounce-back-kid lifestyle.

If any of us is ever going to look for hope, we must have a reason for needing it. Most of the time, that reason involves some hardship that is almost more than we can bear. Although I hope that hardships have not struck your house, I suspect they have in one form or another. Now, you may need to discover hope for your life too.

By "hardships," I am not referring only to car accidents or natural disasters; I am thinking of just about any kind of significant loss that can cause trauma or anguish to a person. You might deem your own life events as calamities, misfortunes, catastrophes, heart-breaks, adversities, tribulations, distresses, hardships, privations, miseries, troubles, conflicts, griefs, sorrows, sufferings, pain, or just plain hard times. Everybody is different, and what would seem like a loss of hope to one person would be easy for someone else.

The difficulty often strikes abruptly. You lose your job. Your friend rejects you. Your spouse or even your beloved pet dies. You send off your precious son or daughter into military service in a war zone. Your church falls apart. Your spouse serves you divorce papers. The economy nose-dives and takes your savings with it. (How did the economic downturn of 2008 affect you? It created some real tragedy for some of my friends.)

Hard times reduce you to your elemental self. You often feel weak. Temptations might assail you, especially the temptation to despair. Joy appears to vanish, and the air around you seems heavy. *Woe* becomes part of your vocabulary, and the grass looks greener just about everywhere except where you are standing (or are curled up in the fetal position). You find it hard to get back up on your feet again every time you get knocked down, let alone to keep on walking forward.

BOTH SIDES NOW

"Both Sides Now" is the name of a folk song from the '60s, and it captures a truth. I can look at life from both sides, which I previously could not do. I have experienced both heaven-sent highs and the bleakest lows—sometimes in the same day. And, firsthand, I have learned some things about God that I did not know before. I have experientially learned that God is the author of hope. God abounds in hope, and he wants to restore the song of your heart. Yes, your heart can beat again!

I have learned that it is okay to be real. Raw reality is better than any mask, especially the pat answers and sugary smiles of religion, which ignore the fact that you may be bleeding to death inside. You will never be healed until you admit that you are sick!

I have learned to live life in the light of eternity, and I can identify with my namesake, James, when he says that life is but a "vapor" (James 4:14 NKJV). That does not mean I am living some kind of pie-in-the-sky existence. It just means that I get it now. I get it. I know both sides of the stormy clouds now, and I know that my faithful, hope-imparting God holds me in his strong hands day and night. I have found that he is bigger than any hardship you or I can cook up in our worst nightmares. He can handle anything, and joy does come in the morning (Psalm 30:5 NKJV). Now I know beyond a shadow of a doubt that:

> Having been justified by faith, we have peace with God through our Lord Jesus Christ, through whom also we have access by faith into this grace in which we stand, and [we can] rejoice in hope of the glory of God. And not only that, but we also glory in tribulations, knowing that tribulation produces

perseverance; and perseverance, character; and character, hope. Now hope does not disappoint, because the love of God has been poured out in our hearts by the Holy Spirit who was given to us. (Romans 5:1–5 NKJV)

I can look at the storm clouds from both sides now, and I can look at life from both sides of the pulpit. I have been a full-time vocational minister now for over forty-five years. I have prayed for people; I have counseled people. I have learned many of the promises that are in the Bible, and I have tried to live up to its character values. But some things I never understood until I went through more than twelve years of what could be considered ongoing trauma. My yardstick of judgment was tossed out the window. Now I understand some things about human frailty. I know what the driving force of pain can make a person do, even though it does not give anyone a license to sin. I did not enjoy the experience of my life spiraling out of control, and I do not like pain any more than the next person—but now I appreciate what God can do with it. I never knew. Now I know.

In the pages that follow, allow me to give you a guided tour of my own triumph in the midst of a roller coaster ride in life. If I can learn new things about God's nature and tell my heart to sing again, then I think you are a great candidate as well. I hope to show you how to discover hope for your journey. I promise to be real because this is not going to touch your heart unless I share from mine.

Are you ready? Here we go onto the path less traveled!

CHAPTER 1

WHEN THE BOTTOM FALLS OUT

Hope deferred makes the heart sick,
but desire fulfilled is a tree of life.
Proverbs 13:12 NASB

While showering after working out at the YMCA one day, I noticed a little nodule. I thought, *Well, that's weird. Never noticed that before. What's that?* I wasn't exactly afraid, but it concerned me enough to go to the doctor. And that took me on a completely unexpected, unasked-for journey.

A stern oncologist did an initial bone marrow exam. The doctor's bedside manner did nothing to soften the impact of neither the test nor the results. I was so unprepared for this to be serious. They did not even take me to another room. They just brought this machine in and started the test. I am sure they anesthetized me, but frankly, I have no recollection of the whole thing. I do remember being scantily clothed (which makes you feel even more vulnerable) and this machine making a buzzing noise. Next thing you know, the doctor is telling me that I have something called non-Hodgkin's lymphoma—cancer.

THE BIG C

I was battling the Big C. Or is it the little c? Yes, it must be the little c because Christ is the Big C, and that proved to be the truth through seemingly endless rounds of treatments.

I remembered a dream I had had earlier, and I realized that God had sent it to fortify me for what was about to happen. In the dream, fierce and foreboding enemies surrounded me. Then my perspective changed, and I rose up so that I could look down on them. My paralyzing terror receded as I viewed these enemies, who now looked like little stick figures. The voice of the Holy Spirit came to me in that dream: *And your enemies shall be like grasshoppers in your own sight*, which echoes a verse from the book of Numbers in the Bible.

Okay, but I still had to fight. Round one involved twenty-five radiation treatments, and they were not pleasant. In fact, it got pretty gruesome. At first, the nodule grew so fast it was the size of a cluster of grapes, and the radiation treatments burned me badly.

I prayed, of course. And people around the world were praying for me. I think I was at the point of about treatment number eighteen when individuals at a gathering prayed over me, and it seemed like the authentic fire of God started flowing through my bloodstream. I had come in with the skin under my clothes blistered and broken, intensely painful and burned from the radiation. By the next morning when I got into the shower, I realized that I had received a miracle. The fiery presence of God had healed my burned skin. I had baby skin where the day before I had looked like a burn victim. I did not have to put special oils on anymore or wear dorky, loose-fitting clothing.

I went back to the radiologist, hoping that I wouldn't have to endure the next scheduled treatments, but they made me complete the whole regimen. It was so great to be healed. But the whole thing was like a roller coaster ride. When it was over, we declared that I was cancer-free, and we had a celebration in the Vanderbilt-Ingram Cancer Treatment Center. And even though we did not really have the money for it, I took my family on a cruise. I had my life back, and my wife, Michal Ann, and I wanted to celebrate in a special way.

WHO TURNED OUT THE LIGHTS?

After a couple of years, I went back to the doctor for a checkup. Unbelievably, the non-Hodgkins lymphoma had come back. Scans showed that it was now located in new places with some growths behind my stomach, which made radiation impossible. I started taking communion every day and doing everything I could to fight the disease. I initiated all sorts of therapies—alternative, naturopathic, praying the Word, soaking in worship, and more. I received lots of prayer, but I was full of questions, and so were the people around me. Why me? What did I do wrong? I tried to figure out if I had opened the door to this somehow, but I really could not find anything. Seriously, how could this be happening? I'd had amazing encounters with God, and he had healed me, hadn't he?

All I could do was keep walking with God and my family, believing that these enemies would yet become like grasshoppers in my sight.

The growth behind my stomach grew some more and then

just sort of went on pause. Then overnight I found a goose egg emerging on my left shoulder. I was then thrust into a second round of passive immunotherapy treatments at yet another hospital. These treatments, in my situation, were even more intense than the first type of therapy, and it ravaged my immune system. All this was happening in the midst of a terrific amount of prayer from people who really know how to pray. But I was internally struggling. How could this be happening to me?

ROUND THREE

Eventually, the growth on my shoulder disappeared, but the growth behind my stomach was just sitting there, rather large and looming. I had half-beaten cancer a second time. Then around Christmas-time, my dear wife, Michal Ann, had severe pain followed by some tests that revealed seven bleeding polyps in her colon. They had to act quickly. She had cancer, too, and they put her in the hospital for major surgery. Now it was as if the bottom of the boat had fallen out. Our four young adult kids (who we always called our miracle kids, but that is another story) had *both* of their parents fighting cancer at the same time.

Michal Ann was plunged into a fight for her life, and she did a magnificent job. Everybody loved her because of her upbeat, positive personality. She was as genuine and unpretentious as they come, an All-American girl who, like me, grew up in rural Missouri. She had never let one negative word be around her, especially now. We were friends; we were lovers; we were partners in ministry. Together, we had founded Ministry to the Nations and then Encounters Network. We had started Women on the Frontlines before she got sick, and then, even after her diagnosis, she launched Compassion Acts, a ministry that pulls together people and other ministries to bring hope to the poor and sick and to victims of political strife and natural disasters. As part of her work with Compassion Acts, she started going on mission trips to southeast Asia and Pemba, Mozambique, to pray for people and to speak at the Iris Ministries school there.

That is where she was when everything came crashing down. I had to phone her to tell her the results of the test the doctors had done just before she left. There she was, eight thousand miles from home, and this wonderfully positive, always-smiling wife of mine just lost it. What a dreadful phone call. I had to tell her that the cancer had re-exploded in her liver, which, in her case, appeared to be a death sentence. By that time, she had already had three organs cut out of her body and she had an ostomy bag, but she thought she had beaten the "little c."

I remember being on that international phone call with her for twenty minutes, and she just sobbed. Seriously, I do not know which was more painful, the physical pain of the cancer itself or the loss of hope. That was one of the worst days of my life, and I'm sure hers as well. We had to say goodbye on the phone and in two different parts of the world. I wrestled with the possibility that we were going to have to say goodbye to the wonderful life as we had known it.

THE LOSS OF MY COMPANION

I will never forget the date in 2008—September 15. Momentously, that is the very date the United States economy tanked. I remember thinking, *A lady knows when to leave.* I will tell you the rest of that story later in this book. Except for that time on the phone, my Annie never surrendered her positive attitude. She never, ever complained. She was never depressed. She always sang praises to her God and kept her smile!

After the dire diagnosis, months passed filled with ups and downs and pain and procedures. Then I lost the only woman I have ever loved, the only woman I have ever been with. We were married for thirty-two and a half years, and we had delighted in our four children, traveled the globe, and written books together. We had prayed together daily, and we knew the true meaning of the word *love*. We had battled our cancers together too, and together we had undertaken every treatment available. But still, the love of my life passed away. Her body was lowered into the ground in a beautiful Dover cemetery in Missouri next to her parents. Her spirit is doing quite well, I know, but as the one left behind, I did not think my pain would ever end.

I am no good with Band-Aids. Some people say I live with my feelings on my sleeve. I am a passionate person, and I live from my heart, which means my joy can be great, but my pain can tear me to pieces. It has not been at all easy to get through this, even sometimes now. Me, a widower? Me, a single parent? I never, ever thought that could happen. Me, in debt? Me, the guy who had never missed a single payment on anything throughout his entire life? I was drowning in three hundred thousand dollars of medical debt. The bottom had fallen out, and I was not sure if I knew how to swim in these uncertain waters.

Living near Nashville, it was as if I was singing one of those mournful country songs: "My wife left me ... my money's all gone... my dog died ..." (By the way, my dog did die after Michal Ann too. after fourteen years of sleeping in our bedroom every night.)

Where was the so-called "abundant life" that Jesus talked about (John 10:10)?

THE GOLDFISH BOWL

I did not want the life I was living, and I would not wish it on any-body. I walked in pain and sorrow and anguish and grief. I hear there are five steps to recover from grief. I think I tried to skip over a couple of them, and I'm not sure I ever reached stage five.

Part of my problem was that I was also a public person living in a public "goldfish bowl" with my children. I had chosen that lifestyle, but my kids had not. None of them had ever volunteered to submit themselves to so much public scrutiny and unsolicited advice. For the most part, people were well-meaning, but nobody likes to have their weaknesses and dilemmas exposed and fixed.

It was as though Job's friends came out of the woodwork wherever I went; people gave me so many different interpretations of where I had gone wrong and what I should do now. I used to say I could find nothing useful in two books of the Bible: Leviticus and Job. Now I felt like Job was my personal friend. I understand that book now and its many twists and turns.

I continued in public ministry. I had to. I had no other means of earning a living. I would go places and preach with my heart either just absolutely dead or hemorrhaging with pain and loneli-ness. As well as I could, I was trying to be faithful and prayerful, to offer up a "sacrifice of praise." I was fragile, and a lot of people lost patience with me. Thankfully, some did not.

Still, I lost 70 percent of the financial contributors that had taken years to pull together. I think some people just thought, *Well, it has to be sin because his wife died and he has fought off can-*

cer at least twice. Maybe some did not want to be associated with someone who was going through such a severe level of attack and calamity. I do not expect to understand what happened with the people who had once stood with me. But I have learned to bless any and all! Job did. So have I.

I HAVE WHAT? AGAIN?

In 2009, a year after Michal Ann graduated to heaven, I found out that my cancer had returned—with a vengeance. The growth behind my stomach had grown to the size of a large baked potato, and the cancer had reached around to the front of my stomach and started going down my right leg. I hardly dared to tell anybody about the extent of it. People had their own lives to live, and surely they were getting tired of hearing from the one some considered "the boy who cried wolf," let alone rallying around me.

Would this affliction ever, ever end? I was still getting prayers. I still believed God. I still did everything I knew how to do to get better and stay healthy.

But I had to find something I did not even realize I had lost—my helmet. Huh? Yes, in the midst of the battle for my life, I had mislaid my helmet of the hope of salvation (1 Thessalonians 5:8). The sixth chapter of Ephesians talks about putting on the whole armor of God, and the helmet is one of the most important pieces of protection. I had to make sure that I positioned my helmet firmly on my head because most of this battle was taking place in my thoughts, in my mind. If I wanted to turn the tide of the battle, I was going to have to get my hope back.

What is hope? According to Mr. Webster, it means to cherish a desire with an expectation of fulfillment. Hope is a confident

anticipation of good. It is not just wishful thinking or thinking posi-
tively. It is not the same as, *Well, I hope so.* Hope is as solid as a
helmet, but no helmet will protect you from danger if you have laid
it aside.

Although my world had crashed, I needed to be able to say
to myself, *Something good is about to happen.* I sure did not feel
like it. I felt abandoned, and I did not know at all how I was going to
make it. I hardly knew where to begin speaking to my own thoughts
and emotions, or how to graft the Word of Life inside myself. I was
going to have to reach deep into God's resources because I did
not have any reserves left within me to keep me moving forward.
I didn't even have much hope anymore because hardships had
crushed it so many times.

HOPE DEFERRED

I started this chapter with the following verse from the book of
Proverbs: "Hope deferred makes the heart sick, but desire fulfilled
is a tree of life" (Proverbs 13:12 NASB). "Hope deferred" means
hope postponed or delayed. That means that something you were
expecting to happen did not happen—or it did not happen as you
thought it would—and that not only makes the heart sick but often
the body and mind too. Hope deferred means more than waiting an
extra day for a Christmas present. Hope is a heart thing, a life-giving thing, and when it falters or sputters out, we stumble, sometimes badly, often feeling as if we might be the only one on the
planet going through such a thing.

Naturally, we can't wait to get to the second part of the proverb: "desire fulfilled is a tree of life." But we always need to start our
journey in the first half of the verse.

BATTLE OF THE HEART

The whole thing is a heart battle. Here is another proverb about that: "Watch over your heart with all diligence, for from it flow the springs of life" (Proverbs 4:23 NASB).

How does it work? If you do a quick study of the "heart" verses, you will find that you can have a dull heart and a slow heart. You can have a hard heart, but you can also have a sensitive, tender heart. Your heart can make you vibrant and vigorous—or robotic and plodding. In order to understand your heart, you do not need to study cardiology. You do need to learn how your spirit operates. I have learned that the only way that I can enjoy life and enjoy God and enjoy the people around me in the present tense is by keeping my heart pumping—even when it hurts to do so.

Three typical responses to pain or rejection deaden our hearts:

1. We move away from people and God.

2. We move toward some other source of relief or acceptance.

3. We move against others.

I probably tried all three ways, and I do not recommend them. In some seasons, I moved away from others and isolated myself. Some people move away from church or family as well. I have moved toward seeming sources of acceptance, sometimes pretty aggressively—forgetting that God's acceptance is all that I need. We all know people in pain who have moved from place to place, even spouse to spouse, looking for fulfillment in all the wrong places. We have such a need to be accepted, to be known and appreciated; we do whatever we feel we need to do to get approval from others.

Then there is bitterness, with which we move against others. The pain settles deeper, and now in addition to isolating ourselves and trying to find acceptance in some *safe* place, we develop judgments against the ones we see as perpetrators of our pain. We move against the community of believers and our families. We may move against God. We get adversarial and then shift over into a victim mindset. Our glass is perpetually half-empty, and no one had better contradict our opinion on that score.

WHAT ARE MY CORE VALUES?

In order to learn to hope again, I had to go back to my ABCs, to my foundations. What did it matter that I was a professional minister who had traveled the globe and ministered in over fifty nations, and had written over thirty books? I had to start back at the beginning. I figured out three core values: (1) God is good, all the time; (2) "All things work together for good to those who love God, to those who are the called according to His purpose" (Romans 8:28 NKJV); and (3) Something good is just about to happen.

Number one, "God is good, all the time," is not just a catchphrase. I read the Bible from front to back all over again, and it convinced me that God just does not make mistakes. He loves me. He loves everybody. He knows what he is doing. We just have to believe that even when we are feeling as if the very life has been snuffed out of us.

"All things work together for good ... " People who feel they must say something helpful in the face of tragedy too often use that scriptural advice glibly. But the fact that it has been overused does not invalidate it. Not that everything that happens is good, but if you continue to walk with him, he will take your broken pieces and mend them supernaturally—and that is an absolute miracle. With him, hope is on the way.

"Something good is just about to happen." That one seems to follow logically from the other two. How in the world can so much tragedy work out for the good? I do not know, but God does. Who can bring light to this dark night of the soul? He can.

HERO OF HOPE: JOB

At the end of each chapter, I will be sharing a short story of someone I feel personifies the theme of each chapter. I trust they will encourage you as they have me, and I highly encourage you to read more on these amazing heroes of hope.

The book of Job tells the story of a man who had amazing tenacity. He kept walking in his integrity even when he lost everything and everybody. Controversy swirled around him, and his wife and friends gave him terrible advice, but he endured. It takes a hero to do that. He didn't really understand God's character until later, but he kept believing in Him.

At the end of Job's story, there is a pivot point. His patience and perseverance (held up in James 5:11 as heroic) is rewarded. Instead of disputing with his friends, he prays for them (Job 42:8, 10). And then good things began to happen again. The end of Job's life was much better than the beginning because the Lord gave him twice as much as he had before and a very long life in which to enjoy it.

Like Job, I had to learn to *redemptively interpret* all the people who wanted to fix me. When I did that, I realized that they just wanted me to be well. They were trying their best to help me get well because they actually cared. So instead of resisting them on the grounds that they could not understand my incomprehensible losses, I began to pray for them and bless them.

So if the bottom has fallen out for you, take a moment to pray with me right now as we begin to rediscover life together.

PRAYER

Father, I present myself to you in Jesus's great name, and I declare that you are the source of my life. In you I live and breathe and have my very being. Take me on a journey to a place where hope is no longer deferred but where fulfilled desire becomes a tree of life. As I come running into your arms of redemptive love, do what only you can do. Only in you can all things be made new. Amen.

DISCOVERING HOPE TAKEAWAYS

Chapter 1
When the Bottom Falls Out

✦ Hope is a confident anticipation of good. Tragedies deprive you of good things and take away your hope.

✦ Hope is vital to your well-being. How can you start to find it again?

- Evaluate your responses to your pain. Get help to find your way past automatic reactions such as bitterness and despair.

- Figure out the core values of your life.

- Put on your "helmet of the hope of salvation" (1 Thessalonians 5:8 KJV), which protects your soul and spirit.

CHAPTER 2

ANYBODY GOT A ROAD MAP?

"For I know the plans that I have for you," declares the Lord,
"plans for welfare and not for calamity to give you a future and a hope."
JEREMIAH 29:11 NASB

Here I was, the guy who used to write books that would explain three hundred Scripture verses, and I could not figure out what to do in the short-term, let alone the long-term. I had lost so much— so many relationships and ministry connections, so much income, even so much sleep—I could hardly keep track of what day of the week it was. It did not take me long to recognize the fact that, before all of this happened, I used to take too much for granted, such as my health and basic contentment. But that realization was not very useful in the present moment when it came to getting through one day after another and especially through the nights. The nights were the worst. My resilience was depleted, and my gifts and credentials did not seem to matter much anymore. I was groping in the dark.

It is impossible to travel safely in pitch-blackness unless you have some kind of navigation system. Even if you are not particularly directionally challenged as I happen to be (I can get lost even on my way to the airport), you can't stay on any road or path in the dark. You need guidance, some kind of GPS to take over. When you are going through a dark night of the soul for whatever reason, it may take a while before you remember that God is your GPS—and that he wants you to have his help.

Has this been your experience? Or do you know in theory that he is your GPS, but you wonder if he knows your name and address anymore? When you go through severe stress, you tend to lose your bearings. You might have always walked with God, but now you barely recall what it was like. You used to be able to follow his directions, but now your road map is lying crumpled in the dirt, and everything around you looks unfamiliar. You feel lost.

To find your way again, you are going to need directions that are super-simple and easy to follow. I did not remember that at first. As I mentioned in the previous chapter, I had to go back and rediscover my core values because they seemed like all I had left. I also decided to lay hold of the "main and plain" doctrines of the faith and to stick with the Word of God. I reviewed the facts: Jesus Christ is the only Son of God. Salvation comes by grace through faith in him. My life matters to him. There is an eternity and a heaven. God's Word has authority. And many more.

But did he really care about me? The minute I allowed myself to wonder if maybe I was an exception to God's Word, I began to flounder again. The enemy takes advantage of our doubts. *Did God really say that? Is anything an absolute truth?* Down I would go. *Well, maybe God does love people in general, but I'm so far from him that I don't think he loves me like he used to. I am just another number.*

I found out that I could not even rely on my memory of what God is like. I had to review the written Word. God's Word is the complete road map for yesterday, today, and tomorrow. But you have to *look* at the map, right now. It is not good enough to have looked at it five or ten years ago. I had to reexamine what it says— each day. I had to stick to it and follow its directions. Once again, the Word of God proved to be a lifeline. I rediscovered that it can show you the way through any wilderness or wasteland you find yourself in.

RUN TO GOD

As I kept reading the Word, I ran across what the disciples had said: "Lord, to whom shall we go? You have words of eternal life" (John 6:68 NASB). They did not have anywhere else to turn, and neither did I.

What makes us think that our pain will go away if we run *away* from God? He is our redeemer. He redeems our lives from destruction (Psalm 103:4)! He gives us a redemptive understanding of our circumstances. Are you lost and miserable? Abandon yourself to him. Run straight into his arms. He will speak the words of life to you. He is your refuge. He is your stronghold of hope. He is always there for you; all you have to do is turn to him and say, *Here I am*.

Make sure you turn to Him and not to somebody else or to something that can medicate your pain. In times of trouble, establish some firm boundaries for yourself. God will never leave you, but you can turn away from him, repeatedly. In your distress and disillusionment, you can resort to old addictions or unhealthy patterns. Many times, people go back to the sources of comfort they knew before they came to Christ. They opt for alcohol, drugs, illicit relationships, pornography, or gambling. They fall back into gossip, blame, shame, strongholds of poverty, and defensiveness. It will be different for every person.

Some people isolate themselves. Others feel they just have to be around other people all the time. They're just trying to lessen the pain somehow, but it means that they are wandering around in the dark until they realize that they need to set their minds and hearts on God alone. Figure out what your personal default setting is and do whatever you need to do to avoid it.

It is no use chafing about the situation. Hard stuff happens, and most of it seems unjust and unwarranted. But God is still good, and he is still there for you. As one of my fathers in the faith told me, "The book of Job is still in the Bible." God has never changed the way life works. What the devil meant for evil, God will always turn for the good.

What does this have to do with *Tell Your Heart to Sing Again*? A whole lot because you can make things much worse than you need to. You will discover hope more quickly if you learn to partner with God.

RUN TO A TRUSTED COMMUNITY

One of the places God's road map will take you is to people you can trust—people who love well. Most of the time, this will include your family. For me, it did; I ran to my kids, who were young adults. "You ran to your *kids?*" you may say. "You are their father!" Well, I tried to lean on them, and I know that sometimes I was a little too much for them. But even though their mother was gone, we were still family, and forgiveness covers a lot of fumbling around. In my case, four kids soon became eight because all four of them got married within a four-year span, and now they are having kids of their own, so I am a grandpa. I will never be a perfect father, but I love my kids like crazy (I talk about them all the time), and they love me back. And we have learned to fight together to maintain a semblance of something called family.

I also ran to my friends. What a gift they are! I owe a lot to Bill Greenman, vice president of my board of directors. That man has a gift of faith. I remember one time I needed a friend with me at one of those intense oncology appointments, and he was there for me. And when I had to have serious back surgery in June of 2014 (which I haven't told you about yet), he and a few other trusted friends were the ones who chauffeured me around for more than four and a half months when I could not drive.

I am so thankful for my dear friend Mickey Robinson, who has a strong gift of encouragement, like Barnabas. He survived a plane crash many years ago, and the strength he received from God and others he now shares with his friends. He checks on me, and I appreciate him so much. He is the brother I never had.

I want to give a big shout out to Chester and Betsy Klystra, founders of Restoring the Foundations, who took me under their wings and provided a safe place of processing and healing for me. Every other month for a year, I drove to Hendersonville, North Carolina, to hang out with these compassionate, skilled practitioners. I was not a "number" to them. I was a broken man within whom they saw the gold of God. My soul can never say thank you enough.

You do not have to have dozens of friends when you have a few really good ones. In fact, four will be enough to carry your cot and to help get you into the presence of Jesus (Mark 2:4; Luke 5:19). At some point in time, you will need to be one of the four carriers yourself, and at other times, you will need their help.

Run to people who love you and who are able to bring you into the presence of the Lord. God has blessed me with the counsel of those who are older and wiser in the faith, such as "Papa" Don Finto, who is now in his late-eighties. That man "loves the hell out of people," and that is a direct quote. I wish everybody could have someone like him to talk to when going through hard times.

You may be saying, "Well, that's nice for you, James, but I don't have anybody like that." I would say back to you, "You have the greatest friend in the world, and he is right with you day and night." Ask Him to come to you. I had a period of about a month when the Holy Spirit would wake me up in the morning with a different secular song. One morning, for example, it was James Taylor's song "You've Got a Friend," which says that when nothing's going right and you are "down and troubled," needing a helping hand, you have a friend. I knew who my friend was! Someone to help me "climb every mountain"!

Maybe it is true that you do not have family to run to, and your friends turning on you (like Job's) has eroded your trust. But even if you have good people in your life as I do, they cannot really meet your deepest needs anyway. My kids could not meet my needs, and I had to come to grips with the reality that I could not meet theirs. At the end of the day, friends can never fully meet your needs. Just remember to call out the name of Jesus, and the greatest brother and friend of them all will come to you. He believes in you, and He knows what to do.

WORSHIP WITH YOUR QUESTIONS

You do not have to call out to Jesus in a proscribed way, using special religious language. You certainly do not have to figure yourself out beforehand. When you call out to Jesus, you can bring anything to him, even your unresolved questions. It can be a form of actual worship.

Worship God with your *questions*? You would want your questions answered, wouldn't you? Yes, but I have discovered that one of the best ways to get them answered (and quickly) is to entrust them to him in worship. Worship him by trusting him with your biggest, messiest questions. Tell him you do not know the answers, but you know he does, and you will wait in full expectation for something good to come. He wants you to do this, whether you bring him some big philosophical or religious question or (more than likely) some emotion-laden practical thing.

Here is an example: My wife had some horses, and somebody needed to keep taking care of them after she died. My youngest son sacrificially went down to the barn and fed the horses every day for the entire first year when I just could not emotionally go down there. That barn represented so much pain for me because it was a place Michal Ann so cherished. I could not stand that barn because she had loved it and found so much intimate life with God in that broken-down barn. For me, her dream place was now my death trap.

Then the time came when I just had to get over it. I went down there for about an hour, hay allergies and all. I fed the horses. My eyes watered, my nose ran, and I hated every minute of it. I went again, and it did not get any easier. I remember the day I went to the barn and crawled up into the loft that was full of hay. I was simply overwhelmed. I opened the hayloft doors, and I just started screaming. I wept a whole lot too. I needed to let it out and express my feelings, and I decided that God was safe enough to take it. I found out that he was not the least bit offended when I told him how much I hurt and could not stand that barn.

I don't remember what I yelled, but I can tell you that it was not "I hate you" or anything like that. I just screamed my pain. And guess what? My scream of pain turned into praise. I just started thanking God for those horses and for that barn. I started thanking God for that stinking hay. I did not understand it all, but when I turned all of my unanswered questions into praise, I could begin to offer a true sacrifice of praise. I stood right there on the edge of the loft floor peering thru open doors looking out onto what once was our "field of dreams." From that loft perch of that sacred barn, I started to thank the Lord!

True worship comes from the heart. I learned how to take care of the barn and the horses. (I tried anyway.) And I learned to love that place. Enjoy it, even. It became a place of healing for me. Worshiping in one of the places of my greatest pain enabled me to trust him with all my heart. Oh, the agony and the ecstasy!

Trusting means not leaning on my own understanding (Proverbs 3:5–6). And out of that comes hope and a certain amount of joy. I might never understand the answers to all my questions on this side of heaven, but one day, I will. The reality is that, right now, we all see through a mirror dimly (1 Corinthians 13:12), and sometimes the only way to worship is to worship God with our questions.

THE IMPORTANCE OF FORGIVENESS

Along with being real with my painful, unresolved questions and working them through with God's help, I had to forgive a lot. I cannot overstate the importance of forgiveness, which is a prominent part of Jesus's message. I mentioned feeling as though Job's friends surrounded me as people pressed in with their unwelcome advice. Would it have helped to express my exasperation to them and to drive them away? Was that what Job did? Well, no. With God's help, Job prayed for his friends (Job 42:8, 10). He blessed them even though he had not experienced much blessing from their interference. In a similar way, I took it upon myself to forgive the "Job's comforters" around me for their heavy-handed efforts, and I blessed them. Repeatedly, I released them from my judgment. I allowed gratitude to take over.

On top of that, I had to forgive myself for the self-imposed expectations that I had not met. That may sound a little crazy, but it worked. I had taken a beating, and I had fallen for too many discouraging lies about myself. As a result, I found myself in sort of a cul-de-sac, going nowhere. In forgiving myself, I let him be my Savior again. Forgiveness was like putting the key into the ignition of my stalled life.

Forgiveness is a choice. I did not have to *like* what had happened. I just had to forgive myself and others, and then I could turn around. I could turn back to God, and then he could minister new life to me. Nobody could do it for me, and I couldn't do it for anybody else, including my kids. I just had to turn away from the gripey, "woe is me" attitude and affirm that God is the source of my life. Yes, in him I live and move and have my being (Acts 17:28). I told him that I would follow him wherever he took me. I remembered that Jesus's disciples had to make that decision too, and that he had led them into some pretty intense stuff. I wanted to follow Jesus, even if it meant more pain. I never wanted to hear my Lord say, "You do not want to go away also, do you?" (John 6:67 NASB).

Somehow—and I do not think any of us understands quite

how this works—practicing forgiveness leads directly to a restoration of hope. Fact stated. Period!

PICTURES OF HOPE

In the Book of Hebrews, we find hope pictured in two ways—as a place of refuge and as an anchor:

> Therefore, we who have fled to Him for refuge can have great confidence as we hold to the hope that lies before us. This hope is a strong and trustworthy anchor for our souls. It leads us through the curtain into God's inner sanctuary. Jesus has already gone in there for us. He has become our eternal High Priest in the order of Melchizedek.
> (Hebrews 6:18–20 NLT)

We can hold onto hope as the fugitives used to hang onto the horns of the altar in the ancient Israelite cities of refuge (Numbers 35). In those days if someone sinned in a way that made him liable to punishment under the law, he could run to a designated city of refuge and he would be safe. God is our city of refuge; when we run to Him, we can grab hold of hope.

Hope will secure our emotions, which crash like wild waves inside our souls and threaten to drown us. Hope is the strong and trustworthy anchor for our souls. In an unstable, impermanent, ever-changing world, hope fastens us to the bedrock of God, the Rock of Ages. Within the sanctuary of God, anchored firmly on Him, we are safer than ever—safer, believe it or not, than before the storm engulfed us.

HEROINE OF HOPE: REBECCA SPRINGER

I am building my own hall of heroes, something like the list of saints in Hebrews 11 (the "faith hall of fame"). Putting this together is part of my journey, and I want to share with you what I have discovered. Besides Job, I discovered another hero: a woman named Rebecca Springer. She lived from 1832 to 1904, and she wrote a Christian book called *Intra Muros* (Latin for *Within the Walls*), which has been revised and published under slightly different titles over the years. The version I have is called *Within Heaven's Gates*, and my eldest son gave it to me in hopes of providing me some help and perspective. I liked it so much I gave copies of this amazing book to all four of my kids the first Christmas after Michal Ann's death.

Rebecca Springer was the daughter of a Methodist clergyman, and she attended Wesleyan Female College, graduating at eighteen. Then she married William, a lawyer who was a member of the Illinois General Assembly. At one point in her life, Rebecca was in failing health herself, and she almost died. She did not die though. Instead, God took her on an extended journey to heaven, which she recorded in this book.

In her accounts, she tells about a riverside where you can go and meet loved ones who have preceded you to heaven. For a person who has lost someone precious, it is profoundly hope building to hear about how we are going to be separated only for a while. And it is so good to realize that since we will one day meet on the other side, we should continue to live a full life here.

My youngest daughter was so moved by reading this account that she composed a touching song about this reality and recorded it with her producer husband. The transparent song is aptly called "Waterside," and it is one of the most impactful tracks from their

August York recording. Yes, we might feel as if we are swimming upstream and just trying to keep our heads above water when the bottom falls out. But there is a day that we will meet again at the shore on the other side.

Rebecca Springer is a heroine of hope to me because she gives me an eternal perspective on the losses I have suffered already as well as on those yet to come. I do not expect to duplicate her experience of visiting heaven while I am still alive, but reading about her experience gives me a very real road map to follow—because, as we know, the narrow and winding road to heaven starts right here on earth, and it can be all too easy to wander from it.

PRAYER

Father, instead of masking my pain, I bring it to you. I choose to worship you with my questions. I believe that Jesus came to heal the brokenhearted and to set at liberty those who are oppressed (Luke 4:18). I present my past, my present, and all that I hope to be—my future—to you. I choose to believe that you have a hope-filled plan for the rest of my life. Gracious Lord Jesus, thank you! Amen.

DISCOVERING HOPE TAKEAWAYS

Chapter 2
Anybody Got a Road Map?

✦ God is the only one who can help you navigate your dark journey—and he wants to help you.

✦ How can you find the hope that is both a place of refuge and an anchor (Hebrews 6:18–20)?

- Run to God and run to trusted people.
- Worship God with your unanswered questions.
- Forgive.

CHAPTER 3

CATCHING THE LITTLE FOXES

Great is Your faithfulness.
"The Lord is my portion," says my soul,
"Therefore I hope in Him!"
LAMENTATIONS 3:23–24 NKJV

One bleak day, my EQ (Emotional Quotient) was at rock-bottom. I do not remember how many of my kids were home that day, but I felt so overwhelmed that I retreated to the privacy of my bedroom and began to sob uncontrollably. Before long, weeping even harder, I went into my bathroom and shut the door. What I really wanted to do was to crawl into a hole in the ground and never come out, but that was impossible. So to put as much distance between myself and my painful situation as I could, I went through the only remaining door, which led to my walk-in closet.

With three doors between me and the rest of the house, I thought maybe I could hide from not only my family but also from God. But thanks to my oldest daughter, whose bedroom was on the second floor right above me, I was not allowed to self-destruct for long. I wish everyone could have someone like this tenacious young adult of mine, someone who can get in your face with tough love.

Thinking I had isolated myself completely, I was startled to hear a little knock on the door of the closet. "Dad?" The light switched on as she let herself in. "Dad, you seem to think we are the only family going through tragedy, but we are not. Everybody goes through difficulty at some point in life."

One moment I was beside myself with hopeless grief, and the next moment I was confronted with reality—by someone who cared enough to seek me out. What's more, this someone was not afraid to break up my pity party and tell me what to do. Next I heard, "You think that we are elite and that we're above this, but we are not. You just have to get over this!"

STOP THE WORLD!

Not that it was easy to get over this. I just wanted it to stop. Many days, I did not want to even get out of bed in the morning. I just wanted to pull the covers up over my head and pretend that nothing had happened. Of course, that is called "denial," and it is not as safe as it would seem under the covers. What was it that Jesus said? "You will know the truth, and the truth will set you free" (John 8:32 NIV). *Truth,* not denial, would set me free.

For the first year after Michal Ann graduated to heaven, I kept a private journal called "Dear Annie" so that I could keep processing my emotions and sorting out the situation with as much of God's light as I could manage. One day, I wrote, *Could we just stop the world from spinning today? I am not quite sure how much more of this spin I can take. Stop the world—I want to get off!* I was spiraling downward into thought patterns that I never dreamed I would get into. I had been walking with my best friend Jesus since I was three years old, but now I felt I was losing touch with him. I knew this happened to other people, but I never expected it to happen to me. I *knew* the truth! Or did I? I began to turn over every stone in my mind.

As may always be the case, the little issues added up and attempted to pull me under. Emotionally, I was so close to the tipping point that small slights and disappointments, which would never have bothered me otherwise, would crush me. I felt like a pot of simmering water on the stove that had been heated to almost the boiling point; all it took was one little thing more and I would spill over. Everything came into play: my particular mix of gifts and sensitivities, my background and experiences, the culture I grew up with, even my birth order.

All of us are different, but we all have a tipping (or boiling) point. What we do not know about ourselves can hurt us—and others. It takes hard experience to learn how to turn down the heat in the midst of our distress.

ONE THOUGHT LEADS TO THE NEXT

The reason behind the title of this chapter, "Catching the Little Foxes," has to do with the sneaky way little harmless issues can accumulate and bring you down. It comes from a line in the Song of Solomon: "Catch us the foxes, the little foxes that spoil the vines, for our vines have tender grapes" (Song of Solomon 2:15 NKJV). We need to capture those fox-like little thoughts before they ruin everything we have worked so hard to cultivate.

The first little fox tiptoes into your troubled mind and makes you think, *I feel so alone.* Then, *Worse, I feel cut off ... In fact, I feel utterly rejected ... I'm just a piece of discarded trash as far as everyone, including God, is concerned ... I don't think there's a place for me in the body of Christ ... My future is ruined.*

You know who sends these foxes, don't you? The devil himself, the one who is skilled at wrapping the truth in a lie. Yes, you feel alone. But after you give in to that sad, temporary truth, the lies start to roll in. Cut off? Rejected? Discarded trash? That is false! The only one it holds true for is, in fact, the devil himself. He's the one who has been cut off and rejected, not you. He just wants your company, and he does *not* wish you well. The devil is the one who has no future in the body of Christ, not you. He is the hopeless one, not you, and he is attempting to lure you into his lair so he can eat you for lunch. Resist him!

> Stay alert! Watch out for your great enemy, the devil. He prowls around like a roaring lion, looking for someone to devour. Stand firm against him, and be strong in your faith. Remember that your family of believers all over the world is going through the same kind of suffering you are.
> (1 Peter 5:8–9 NLT)

One of his oldest tricks is to speak in the first person. He plants those thoughts in your mind, and you think they are truly your own. *I feel so bad today ... It's downhill from here ... I'm never going to be happy again.* You swallow these lines because they seem to apply so accurately to your situation. It does not occur to you to counter them with scriptural truth. You are thinking, *I feel so cut off from God.* But if you are in Christ Jesus, you are not cut off—you have been grafted into the family of God with full access to the throne of grace to receive help and mercy in time of need (Hebrews 4:16).

You do not have to stay where you are. Just because the devil lured you into a downward spiral of thinking does not mean you have to stay down there. Even though you may carry some unhealed hurts from the past or some unforgiveness, that should not relegate you to a condition of hopelessness. What went spiraling downward *can* be turned around. You can spiral up too. You can take one step after another onto a succession of truths until you come back up to where you can breathe God's pure air again. Yes, you can! All things are possible.

Romans 12:2 urges us to *renew* our minds. With the help of the Holy Spirit, your thinking can be transformed so that you can "prove what is that good and acceptable and perfect will of God" (NKJV). If you are able to *prove* something, it must be true. What is that good and acceptable and perfect will of God? That must be something worth hoping for. The specifics will vary, but it will be good. And remember, hope is the happy anticipation of something good. Your hope is back. You thought it was gone forever, but your Savior sought you out.

THE GOOD SHEPHERD

Jesus, the Good Shepherd, leaves the ninety-nine sheep that are okay for the moment to go off in search of the ones that are isolated and in danger. This is not just a nice metaphor from the Bible (Matthew 18:12). It remains true today, and I know it firsthand. I have never backslid, walking away from the Lord and my faith, but for sure I have needed saving. When I was broken, I felt lost. My own efforts did not work. I was "prone to wander" as the old hymn says. I was going off course in my thoughts and straying down the path of remorse.

Most important, the Good Shepherd is the one who sought me out. It did not depend on my own efforts. He loved me even when I had backed myself into a cul-de-sac, and he still had a wonderful plan for my broken life. Although my own faith was weakened, he came looking for me with open arms. He is absolutely faithful all the time.

Besides being faithful, he loves us. And he is in charge of the situation—if I will let him be in charge. I have to choose to follow him. And so do you. The Bible says, "Choose today whom you will serve" (Joshua 24:15 NLT). Will I choose to serve old thought patterns or new ones? Will I choose to replace those little foxes with God's truth?

> Whatever things are true, whatever things are noble, whatever things are just, whatever things are pure, whatever things are lovely, whatever things are of good report, if there is any virtue and if there is anything praiseworthy—meditate on these things. (Philippians 4:8 NKJV)

If I am his and he is in charge, I am not a victim. I can pick up my helmet of the hope of salvation and win this round of the battle. I can turn to comfort others with the comfort I have received from God (2 Corinthians 1:3–5). We can transform into a triumph the very thing the devil meant for evil.

TRIUMPH OVER EVERY TRAUMA

We can find healing for all of our traumas in the love of our Savior. Our current difficulties tap into unhealed and unresolved traumatic events of the past. Every one of our memories carries with it a stored emotion, and a lot of these emotions are undesirable and damaging if we do not catch them, like marauding foxes, and bring them to Jesus's feet.

You walk into a room and a familiar smell triggers a memory. Suddenly you have to review the truth and ask for God's help again. For me, this happened a lot in my bedroom at home, the same bedroom where I watched my dear wife pass from this life to the next. For five years after her death, that room would painfully stir my emotions. I found it easier to be on the road in some hotel room that held no memories for me.

I did not know what to do about it at first. But after a while, I learned to take my painful memories directly to Jesus. I also had to rise up in faith and take authority over the usurper and shut down his lies. After all, Jesus is the great healer. He will heal our emotions and our minds, but we must cooperate with the healing process. Trauma and suffering walk hand in hand with each other, but I found out that I had no obligation to hold hands with them. I could march them to Jesus. He never waved a magic wand to make them disappear, but he always did something better—he transformed the suffering into faith and strength.

He will do it for you too. It is what our God does best. Now you have to do your part, but I tell you the truth, he will do more than his share. He will show you which doors to shut and which doors to open. He will touch each open wound with his presence and heal it—and often he will make sure to leave enough of a scar so you will remember what he has done. Most of all, he will restore your hope.

CHANGE HOW YOU THINK

If you believe that Jesus is your Good Shepherd and that he is looking out for you right now, you can expect him to restore your soul, which includes your mind and your emotions. The best way to cooperate with this is to immerse yourself in his Word and allow it to plant itself deep inside you. You could call it "Word grafting." Psalm 23 is a good place to start. As many people over the centuries have discovered, it is a "psalm for living":

> The Lord is my shepherd; I shall not want.
> He makes me to lie down in green pastures;
> He leads me beside the still waters.
> He restores my soul; He leads me in the paths of righteousness for His name's sake.
> Yea, though I walk through the valley of the shadow of death, I will fear no evil; for You are with me; Your rod and Your staff, they comfort me.
> You prepare a table before me in the presence of my enemies; You anoint my head with oil; my cup runs over.
> Surely goodness and mercy shall follow me all the days of my life; and I will dwell in the house of the Lord forever. (NKJV)

He restores your soul. He gives rest—even peaceful, refreshing sleep in times of high anxiety. He helps you obtain good physical nourishment. He enables you to keep on walking, one step in front of the other. He does it because he is the Good Shepherd. He is not holding you to extraordinary expectations for performance. Victory is defined differently in different seasons of life. Sometimes, just to keep inching forward through the valley of the shadow of death is an absolute victory. Staying on your feet and following him is a victory. Paths of righteousness are not always particularly smooth.

The Good Shepherd wants to be with you, and he is working overtime to seek you out. If you feel the way I did, you may not know yet whether you want him to find you. In the early weeks of my time of deep loss and sorrow, I was ministering in Seoul, South Korea. I was so dead inside that I did not know if I ever wanted to preach again in my lifetime. But I was one of the recognized and somewhat well-known speakers, and I was expected to come up with something. Desperately, I prayed, *Oh God, help me!* And he did.

He turned my attention to the living Word of God, both the written Word and the living Word that dwells inside me. The living Word brings resurrection power. Drawing on the resurrected life of the One who lives inside of me, I got out my notes, picked up my Bible, and made myself walk to that podium in a packed auditorium with my Korean translator. I gave it everything I had, and I preached on something like "Contending for Your Prophetic Promise," even though I felt I had completely lost mine.

After that message, a significant international leader told me, "James, that was the best job of preaching I have ever heard you do." What a miracle! I still felt dead, but I knew God was alive inside of me. God was at work to do his will and his great pleasure in and through me.

It confirmed what I had learned a long time before: that the life I live is not my own but his. And he will take care of me, restore me, refresh me, and even allow me to bless others—all *because of* the unbearable suffering. That restores my soul, my faith, and my hope. As the Word explains in Lamentations (the verse I placed at the beginning of this chapter): "The Lord is my portion," says my soul, "Therefore I hope in Him!"

My soul will speak ("… *says* my soul …"), whether out of its despair or out of its hope and the repository of the implanted

Word. That is why the apostle James wrote, "Therefore ... receive with meekness the implanted word, which is able to save your souls" (James 1:21NKJV). Our souls need saving not only from hell but also from the many dark attacks that may come our way in the course of life. Surely, goodness and mercy will come our way because the Lord is so faithful. He changes everything for better.

HEROINE OF HOPE: JOAN HUNTER

Joan's parents, Charles and Frances Hunter, were known as the "Happy Hunters" because of their joy-filled approach to their decades-long charismatic healing ministry. But the daughter of the Happy Hunters was not too happy. She had never known her biological father, but when she was fourteen, her mother married Charles, and she spent the rest of her growing-up years as part of the well-known international ministry family. Joan later attended Oral Roberts University, where she met and married a young man. Together, they founded and co-pastored a church and had four beautiful children.

Then, after twenty years of marriage, her husband came home one day with his same-sex partner. They ran off together, abandoning Joan and the children. Divorce followed. Joan felt she had a big "D" written on her forehead. Not only did it stand for Divorce but also for Disappointment, Despair, Debt, and a lot more, none of it happy.

The ministry of her mother and stepdad had taught her about divine healing from physical ailments. Now she reached out for herself to the God of all hope and healing, and he taught her about healing for the soul. Today, she has remarried, and she has a reputable, miraculous ministry of her own. She brings God's healing to people by asking the Holy Spirit to help identify the hidden roots of trauma and emotional disruption and then often, along with the emotional and spiritual healing, quickly comes physical healing.

I know Joan well; she is one of my friends. And she is a heroine of hope to me because she did not let the enemy keep her down. She believes and imparts to others the truth that God has a good future in mind for each one of his children and that hope in Him is always fulfilled.

PRAYER

Father, I choose to believe that I am not a victim but that I can be victorious in Christ Jesus. I put my life into your hands. Help me to catch the little foxes that spoil the vine. Restore me from all effects of emotional trauma and abuse. I choose to believe that all things are possible. Now turn my sorrows into places where your abounding grace has the final say. For the glory of God and in Jesus's name. Amen.

DISCOVERING HOPE TAKEAWAYS

Chapter 3
Catching the Little Foxes

✦ When overwhelmed with loss, it's easy to want to shut down.

✦ To receive God's help and help from others, you must catch the fox-like thoughts that threaten to undo you.

- Watch out for downward spirals of thinking.
- Ask God to heal your memories.
- Practice "Word grafting"—immersing yourself in the Word of God so that it takes root in your heart and changes how you think and respond.

CHAPTER 4

METAMORPHOSIS: THE PROCESS OF CHANGE

For there is hope for a tree, if it is cut down, that it will sprout again,
and that its tender shoots will not cease.

JOB 14:7 NKJV

I was with my wife all four times she gave birth, and I learned that there is a crucial time in the final stages of labor called *transition*. For the first two births, I don't remember any major problems. But with number three, she got stuck in the transition stage, and it was not easy. It's supposed to be a short period of time although it is often the most painful stretch. Michal Ann's labor was progressing right along when suddenly it stalled. She and the baby were caught there for almost an hour.

I was trying to do my cool, calm, and collected thing—soothing little washcloth on her forehead, spooning a few ice chips into her mouth, steadying encouragement ("Let's focus. C'mon, focus").

But Mrs. Together just lost it. She started screaming, "I-can't-do-this! I can't!"

I wanted to say, "I think you can because you've done it twice before," and "Really, it's too late to quit now." But I knew better than to make a joke. I couldn't help her, and she couldn't help herself. Then the doctor had to go out of the room for a moment, and right as he came back in—bam!—he got there just in time to catch the baby. Even though her transition had stalled, our third son was born screaming and quite healthy, and his mother's hard labor was over. In its own way, his birth happened perfectly.

TRANSITION TIME

When you find yourself in any kind of transition, especially a prolonged one, it can seem too hard to bear. You just do not think you will make it. You wish you could go back to the way things used to be before all of this pain started. The pressure can be intense, and you feel squeezed from every side, stripped, unprepared. Yet a time of transition is taking you somewhere. Although the passage is narrow, it is taking you from a place of confinement to a place of enlargement. To keep from stalling, you need to let go of the past and allow yourself to propel forward.

In my time of pain and transition, I heard those exact words, repeatedly: *Let go. Let go.* I could seek the Lord for words to encourage others, and he would speak to me. But when I sought him for a word for myself, all I heard from the Holy Spirit was, *Let go.* For at least five years! I had to go through an "Isaac" experience (Genesis 22); I had to be willing to lay everything on the altar. God tested my faith to the limit. I felt I hardly had anything left to surrender, and sometimes, out of sheer obedience, I did just "let go."

I found out that letting go is healthy. Surrender is not the same as defeat; it just means relinquishment of the familiar ways. If I was going to be able to enter into the new phase of my life, I had to let go not only of unhealthy patterns, but also of the old, familiar things that were good, such as my marriage. Even the good can sometimes be an enemy of the best.

I used to think that transition was an abnormal state, but I found out that it is completely normal. I used to think that if only I could get through a difficult season of transition, I would be home free. Well, guess what? When you get through one transition, there will be another one waiting for you. We need to be realistic about it.

In literature, a transition is the bridge between one theme or chapter and the next. It is helpful. It gives you perspective on what will be coming in the near future, and it builds on what came before. So if you feel that you may be coming to the end of a chapter of your life and you are entering into in a time of transition, that means that there is something new for you just over the horizon. Knowing that builds hope.

How you respond during a time of transition is all-important. Years ago, a wonderful mentor told me that what happens to you is not as important as *how you respond* to what happens to you. Are you going to keep moving forward, or are you going to let your fear of the unknown hold you back? Are you going to make excuses for yourself or are you going to press through the emotional storms until you reach the other side?

Sometimes you may feel that change has mowed you down because life as you knew it has ended. But if you pay attention, you can find hope in unlikely places. For example, the verse from Job at the beginning of this chapter seemed new to me when I found it. I do not know where that verse was hiding during the many times

I had read through the book of Job earlier because I do not have any recollection at all of reading it: "For there is hope for a tree, if it is cut down, that it will sprout again, and that its tender shoots will not cease." I am so glad the Holy Spirit directed me to this verse, and I wish I had seen it about eight years before because it is such a graphic portrayal of hope.

If there is hope for a tree, there can be hope for me. As long as the roots are intact, the tree can grow anew, and so can I. This is true not only for trees that get chopped off at ground level but also for fruit-bearing trees and vines that get pruned, sometimes drastically, in order to increase their health and yield. Right after a pruning, the tree or vine might not look too great. But remember what Jesus said: "Every branch that bears fruit He prunes, that it may bear more fruit" (John 15:2 NKJV). The trees that bear the most fruit are the ones that we prune from top to bottom.

TRANSITION FROM A REDEMPTIVE PERSPECTIVE

I am trying to redeem "transition" from being a dirty word in your vocabulary. I want to help you redeem the whole process so that you will be able to find your way through a time of drastic change—with hope. I can see at least eight steps in the process of transition and change:

1. **A desire for change stirs.** You may not be strongly aware of this step, although you may recognize in retrospect that you had developed a longing for something different. Sometimes you just may feel somewhat bored with your life and you want something different, something more.

2. **A new level of revelation comes.** Your desire for

change spurs you to search your heart and to seek God (*What do I really want?*). Inspiration begins to come. A new concept may occur to you, or your search may renew an old dream.

3. **Your present vision adjusts.** The new begins to replace the old, and you become willing to make changes in your life. You start to look at life through a fresh lens, you get a new perspective, and it alters your vision.

4. **You receive grace.** You position yourself humbly under the mighty hand of God where you will have the ability to receive his grace. Recognizing that you cannot achieve anything by your own efforts, you learn to rely on his grace.

5. **Grace heals your past issues.** God's grace brings healing to any number of pertinent unresolved issues, and you begin to see some benefit in the midst of your suffering. What you are going through is turning out to be worth something, and your hope grows.

6. **You grasp a new identity.** In this new season, what role does God want you to play? In relation to others, will you be a leader, a follower, a boss, an employee, a friend, a parent, a spouse? Will you be active, or is God putting you on pause? Your basic identity in Christ will stay the same, but something new will always enhance it. You cannot live just on yesterday's laurels; move on!

7. **You have strength to overthrow your new enemies.** With the combination of God's grace and your new identity, you will have a surge of fresh energy. Your strength

will renew like that of an eagle (Isaiah 30:41). New challenges (enemies) will come along with your transition to a new place in life, and God will give you strength to meet them.

8. **You grasp your new identity.** You stride into your new land with confidence, and you secure it. This may take a while, but you will get there if you persevere. One little step at a time is all it requires.

The whole process depends on *trust.* Are you trusting God? Or are you trusting yourself or your circumstances or other people? Of course, the goal is to put your trust in God alone because he uses every transition to make you more like him. That is the essence of what Paul wrote: "And we all, who with unveiled faces contemplate the Lord's glory, are being transformed into his image with ever-increasing glory, which comes from the Lord, who is the Spirit" (2 Corinthians 3:18 NIV). Believe me, becoming more like him is a wonderful thing, even a glorious thing—like being reborn!

One of the keys for moving forward through a time of transition is to get your eyes off yourself and your often-miserable circumstances. I know that can be much easier to say than do, but it happens by your choosing it, with God's grace. You need to follow Paul's advice and keep your eyes on heaven. This means no navel-gazing. As long as my chin is on my chest, all I can contemplate is myself. But if I lift my gaze toward God, I am transformed in the process.

As the psalmist wrote, "I will lift up mine eyes unto the hills, from whence cometh my help" (Psalm 121:1 KJV). Look up! Suddenly, his beauty strikes you, and you are amazed. *Lord, you are wonderful! You are my redeemer. I don't always understand you, but I trust you with all my heart. I love you. I want to lift my eyes to you in worship, even in the midst of these unresolved internal conflicts. I lay them at your feet.*

I think of the old chorus: "Turn your eyes upon Jesus, look full in His wonderful face, and the things of earth will grow strangely dim, In the light of His glory and grace."

LESSONS LEARNED FROM A WORM

Believe it or not, the life cycle of a worm—a caterpillar—has profound lessons for us, more than you would think. At first, he's just a little thing, crawling around in the dirt by himself. He finds something to eat, and he grows bigger. This is the whole of life as far as the worm is concerned. But changes are coming, and soon the worm will find out that he was destined for something exciting. A new identity is stirring, although at first it certainly does not look like it. The worm feels like climbing upward, so he does. He will never be able to articulate it, but he is beginning to feel stirrings—to fly, of all things! It's compelling. Could he have been born for this? Could you and I have been born to soar far above the valley of despair, up into the heavenly places with Christ?

For the worm, this is transition time, and it isn't pretty. The transition of a caterpillar is called metamorphosis, and I have been interested in this process since I was a boy growing up in tiny Cowgill, Missouri (population 259), where there is precious little to do on a hot summer day except collect bugs and caterpillars. Back then, I learned the rudiments about metamorphosis, and ever since then, I have remained interested in what this process involves. Painting with broad strokes, here are the stages of what happens, in sequence:

First comes a time of normal feeding and growth. The caterpillar eats his fill of leaves or other sustenance, just as we eat our fill of the Word of God. As a result, the caterpillar grows so much that he begins to outgrow his outer skin, although inside he still has a capacity for even greater growth.

Soon a desire, an instinct to climb and explore something new, takes hold. That's all the little worm wants to do. So he crawls up and finds a spot and begins to spin a chrysalis (similar to a cocoon) because, lo and behold, that something new is going to involve confinement in a tight space. It is really transition time now. As it turns out, the caterpillar spins his own "changing room," and so do we, by God's grace. Hope-filled and desperate, we spin dreams and ideas, visions and desires. Our time of transition can seem very demanding and confining, indeed. But old limitations must pass away so that the new may come.

Then nothing happens. Or so it seems. The caterpillar is no longer visible to outsiders, and he can no longer look out upon the world; he is in hiding. It is the same with us, although we may need to be jarred loose from unhealthy hiding places sometimes (I am thinking of my walk-in closet). But "he who dwells in the secret place of the Most High Shall abide under the shadow of the Almighty" (Psalm 91:1 NKJV). That is always a healthy hiding place, the secret place of God.

Actually, I prefer the word *chrysalis* to the word *cocoon* because chrysalis reminds me of Christ, and we are in Christ. Once the worm is in his healthy hiding place, all you can see is the chrysalis. It may seem like a resting place, a pause in the action, but there is always a lot going on as the caterpillar transforms into a new creature.

It may surprise you how this works—his body actually liquefies. Depending on the species of insect, it can take from two weeks to many months. That old caterpillar body breaks down into undifferentiated cells that reassemble into a new creation—something with wings that can fly! I am sure you can see the parallels to what happens to us during a time of significant transition. It can seem like a total meltdown, but then something new emerges.

You can never hurry any stage of the process. Even as a butterfly emerges from its chrysalis, it takes its time. First, a little nudge here and there. A bent leg pokes out then pulls back in. You must not help the butterfly get out because the effort required for the process of its emergence builds the strength that the creature will need in order to fly. In the same way, your friends and family can never do your work for you. They can never rescue you from your tight place, and if they try, they may unnecessarily prolong your time of transition. You are the one who must make the effort. You pray and trust and believe that God's grace is sufficient. You are the only one who can press forward and break out of your dark place and into the full light again.

Like a butterfly, you stretch out your crippled new wings. You catch the light of the sun (the Son!). You flex them. They work! And off you go into new adventures like nothing you have ever had before. Like the worm, you have come to believe that you were born to fly!

HERO OF HOPE: MICKEY ROBINSON

This hero of hope is one of my best friends. I remember when I first met Mickey because I had a hard time looking at him. At nineteen years old, he was a part of an elite parachuting team, and others recognized him as a rising star jumping with the best skydivers in the world. During a routine jump, his life changed forever when a fiery plane crash melted his face and mutilated his body. In the hospital, Mickey had a near-death experience, visited heaven, and received a mission to bring a life-giving message of hope back to the earth. He overcame multiple terminal conditions and experienced dramatic, miraculous healings. Shortly after he recovered from the accident, he gave up skydiving for preaching.[2] But he still bears the marks of this traumatic incident.

One time I asked his wife, "I just have to know ... did you marry him before his accident? Or after?"

She said, "After. I never saw the burns or the scars. I saw the man, and I loved him."

And what a man he is. He is not ashamed of his appearance, and he is not ashamed of the gospel of the Lord Jesus Christ. He travels the globe telling his story, and sometimes we have traveled together. During my battle with cancer and the loss of my wife, Mickey was there by my side and that of my family.

Mickey is not only a warm, enjoyable man to be with; he is a modern-day Barnabas, a premier encourager who brings hope to the hopeless everywhere he goes. Out of the fiery furnace of affliction came something far more valuable than the thrill of skydiving, and I find encouragement and new hope every time I talk with him. His life shows me what really matters.

What has happened to Mickey is a perfect example of God's redemptive care and extraordinary transformation, and his life story makes mine look like a walk in the park. This dear man is a modern-day hero of hope! He is a father of four grown children, who are now adults, and grandfather to a growing number of grandkids. His

---

2   You can read Mickey's gripping story in his book *Falling Into Heaven: A Skydiver's Gripping Account of Heaven, Healings, and Miracles.*

testimony has even appeared in secular televised documentaries around the world. Mickey is a walking miracle!

If God can give my friend Mickey such courage and enduring hope in the midst of the total wreckage of his life, of course he can bring hope to me—and you too.

PRAYER

Father, I believe that in Christ all things are possible! Old things do pass away, and new things do come. Take my life and shape it into the next phase of purpose and destiny. Give me the grace needed for letting go of the old to embrace the process of change and to be prepared for the new. Plant desires within me that overcome the obstacles of the past. Heal me. Shape me. Make me into a person who reflects the radiance of the glory that takes me from change to change. For Jesus Christ's sake. Amen.

DISCOVERING HOPE TAKEAWAYS

Chapter 4
Metamorphosis: The Process of Change

✦ Times of great change and adjustment follow tragedies. Will you keep moving forward and pressing through the emotional storms, or will you make excuses for yourself and let your fear of the unknown hold you back?

✦ As you put your trust in God:

- Your perspective adjusts.
- You receive God's grace to let go of the past and start to look forward.
- You begin to grasp a new identity.

CHAPTER 5

THE DOOR OF HOPE

*I will give her her vineyards from there, and the valley of Achor
as a door of hope. And she will sing there as in the days of her youth,
as in the day when she came up from the land of Egypt.*
HOSEA 2:15 NASB

When my cancer reoccurred for the third time, it was more serious than it had been before. Having already tried most of the possible treatments the first two times, I was not sure what kind of help I should pursue. And this time I was facing everything alone because Michal Ann had died the year before. *Oh, God!* I cried. *I need your help so much!*

I had heard of the Cancer Treatment Centers of America, and I knew that their Midwestern Regional Medical Center was in a city in Illinois called Zion. They are a privately owned institution, and I hoped that my insurance would cover their integrative cancer treatment. So I applied for acceptance—and they turned me down. It felt as though they had slammed the door in my face.

Naturally, I could see the scriptural significance of the name

Zion. I also knew that the history of this particular Zion was saturated with healing, having been founded in 1901 by a Scotsman named John Alexander Dowie, who was a controversial evangelist and faith healer. Now it happened to be the location of this hospital I wanted admittance to so badly.

Dispirited and in tears, I was taking a hot shower when I burst out with a prayer: *God, I just want to go to Zion! I just want to go to Zion!* I thought of a line from Michal Ann's favorite psalm, and I recited it from memory: "How blessed is the man whose strength is in You, in whose heart are the highways to Zion!" (Psalm 84:5 NASB). Yes, I wanted to travel to Zion.

Something inside me rose up, and I thought I should try again. It was as though a door of hope had appeared right in front of me. So again I phoned the number of the cancer center. Again they went through all the rigmarole about my insurance and why they could not accept me, but I found out that the woman on the other end of the line was a believer, so I told her I thought God wanted me to be there. She said, "Well, even though it is supposed to be impossible because your insurance will not cover you and the quotas are filled, I will agree with you in prayer because you believe you have an appointment in Zion." We agreed over the phone in prayer, and she said, "Now I am going to resubmit your application." That was on a Friday.

Monday, I got a phone call. A miracle had happened. They had accepted me! The treatment regimen at Zion would be extremely difficult, but they would allow me to go through it. In fact, this was such an extreme treatment that you could only undergo it one time in your entire lifetime. Well, this was in my lifetime, and this was my divine appointment. My youngest daughter and one of her close friends drove from Nashville to the Chicago area to be there with me along with a couple of my sons in the faith. Oh, what a relief!

WALKING THROUGH PSALM 84

Because of Zion, Michal Ann's "life psalm" took on new significance for me. I was still traveling through a deep valley, but I was beginning to believe that blessings lay ahead. I read and reread each line of the psalm:

> How lovely are Your dwelling places, O Lord of hosts!
> My soul longed and even yearned for the courts of the Lord;
> My heart and my flesh sing for joy to the living God.
> The bird also has found a house, and the swallow a nest for herself, where she may lay her young, even Your altars, O Lord of hosts, My King and my God.
> How blessed are those who dwell in Your house! They are ever praising You.
> How blessed is the man whose strength is in You, In whose heart are the highways to Zion!
> Passing through the valley of Baca they make it a spring; the early rain also covers it with blessings.
> They go from strength to strength, every one of them appears before God in Zion.
> O Lord God of hosts, hear my prayer; give ear, O God of Jacob!
> Behold our shield, O God, and look upon the face of Your anointed.

For a day in Your courts is better than a thousand
outside. I would rather stand at the threshold of the
house of my God than dwell in the tents of wicked-
ness.

For the Lord God is a sun and shield; the Lord gives
grace and glory; no good thing does He withhold
from those who walk uprightly.

O Lord of hosts, how blessed is the man who trusts
in You! (Psalm 84 NASB)

I could see that the highway to the freedom and blessing of
Zion passes through (not around) the Valley of Baca, which can be
translated as the Valley of Weeping. That is how I could tell I must
be right on track.

THROUGH THE DARK VALLEY

I have discovered that the Bible is filled with valleys. So is the natural world. In fact, come to think of it, you cannot have a mountain-
top without at least a couple of valleys on each side. The way new
mountains rise up is by means of great cataclysms and prolonged
erosion in the valleys that are left behind.

Everyone is familiar with the "valley of the shadow of death"
in Psalm 23. Another significant scriptural valley is the Valley of
Achor, which is a place of trouble and distress (that is what the
word *achor* means). It was named after the sinner Achan, who was
stoned to death and buried in that exact valley in Joshua's time
(Joshua 7:26). It appears again in the prophecies of Isaiah (Isaiah
65:10) and in the verse from Hosea quoted at the beginning of this
chapter.

Are we supposed to be afraid of these valleys? Are they

death traps? Not as far as I can see. In fact, just as the shepherd prepares a bountiful table and green pastures close by the valley of the shadow of death, so does God move a door of hope into position—right in the Valley of Trouble. Right there and nowhere else. The Valley of Trouble becomes a door of hope.

Every one of us will go through dark valleys and troubled times. After we have walked with the Lord long enough, we begin to see the truth that the place of trouble always, always leads to a door of hope. Always. God takes your deepest valley, your Valley of Achor, and he transforms it into a door of hope. After the door of hope, Hosea says, comes joyful celebration: "She will sing there as in the days of her youth, as in the day when she came up from the land of Egypt." We will sing and celebrate as Miriam did when God had worked a miracle and delivered the Israelites from Egypt, right through the midst of the Red Sea (Exodus 15:20).

Too many of us stop in the middle. We can't get even a glimpse of the door of hope, so we sit down. I know; I've done it. But if you believe that the valley is only a way of passage through to the mountain heights, the only logical thing to do is get back up and keep moving again. This means that if you find yourself in a valley right now, *keep on walking.* As you walk, you will be gaining new strength so that you will be capable of climbing the mountain when you get there. And once you get high enough up on the mountainside, your perspective will change about the valley of trouble behind you. You will surely exclaim, *Why, that valley is full of flowers. Just look at them! Look at that rushing brook. Look at that green grass. I must have missed it when I was down there!* You will be so glad you kept walking.

You will echo the exultant final words of Psalm 84: "The Lord gives grace and glory; No good thing does He withhold from those

→keep

who walk uprightly. O Lord of hosts, how blessed is the man who trusts in You!" (NASB).

TOO MANY DOORS

Now I have wrapped that up in a nice, tidy package, haven't I? The valley of trouble becomes a door of hope, and joy follows—one, two, three. It is a lot easier said than done though. How will you know if you are doing it right? Will you recognize the door of hope when you see it? How does it manage to stand out from all the other "doors"?

I had a dream one time in which I went through a single door, and it led into a place like a hospital or hotel—a long hallway with doors on both sides as far as I could see. The Holy Spirit spoke to me in the dream and said, *I have now brought you through a door.*

I said, *Yeah, okay.*

And that door is going to lead you to many doors.

That is often what it feels like, doesn't it? Where are you supposed to go? The time of trauma and trouble has created too many decisions for your foggy brain to handle. You are well aware of the standard advice not to make major life decisions in the midst of a troubled time, but sometimes you have to make them anyway. Even the small decisions (*Should I stay home or go out?*) seem difficult.

Let me assure you: if God's grace has carried you through to this point, he will not abandon you now. Reach out to him. Just lean in. He will give you more grace, lots of mercy, and (best of all) peace. You can decide between those multiple doors by means of his peace. You can ask him for guidance and peace as many times over as you need to. He is the source of all righteousness, peace, and joy (Romans 14:17), and you will be able to distinguish his peace from the false peace that may distinguish some of those doors, such as the false peace of escapism.

You have to understand that it is *good* to have multiple options. One of God's greatest gifts to humans is free will, and a chance to use yours presents itself. You can choose to follow God, or you can choose to figure it out all by yourself. You can even choose to turn away and experiment with forbidden fruit of some sort. Sometimes I think he offers us so many choices because our master wants to hear from us. He wants us to consult him as one friend to another.

You can choose to listen for the Shepherd's clear, calm voice, or you can listen to the clamor of voices around you that want to give you advice. Years ago, Dr. Bill Bright wrote a little tract for Campus Crusade for Christ that said, "God has a wonderful plan for your life." He does have a wonderful plan for your life. The problem is, so do a lot of other people.

But the Lord will help you. God's Word will be a lamp to your feet and a light to your path (Psalm 119:105). He is perpetually in control of everything, and he is more than capable of seeing you through your many decisions. God is omnipotent, omniscient, omnipresent. He is *omni-omni!* He will take care of you. Swamped with decisions and options, you might choose right and you might choose not-so-right. You might choose the right door at the right time, or you might choose it out of timing. But because God causes all things to work together for good for those who love him (Romans 8:28), he will scoop up your mistakes and miscalculations, blend them in with your successes and obedience, and come up with a blessing.

You have to lean into God alone as much as you possibly can. He will always see you through as long as you lean in his direction. I love this proverb: "Trust in the Lord with all your heart, and lean not on your own understanding; in all your ways acknowledge Him, and He shall direct your paths" (Proverbs 3:5–6 NKJV). Lean not on your own understanding. Lean on his. The only reason you may feel a little off-balance (besides the fact that your time of trouble probably still has you reeling) is that when you are leaning, you are putting yourself at some risk of falling. But you already knew that trusting faith is spelled R-I-S-K, didn't you?

You will have to lean close to him, like the beloved disciple John did, in order to hear the desires of his heart (John 13:23–25). Most likely, the Holy Spirit will tell you to do something that will be quite impossible without his divine help. You should take that as good news because, weakened as you are, you are already learning that you can't do much on your own.

GOD'S REDEMPTIVE NATURE

God is in the middle of redeeming you. His whole nature is to be a redeemer. Because of his faithfulness, his patience, his loving kindness, his mercy, and his grace, he is bringing you through that doorway labeled "Hope." God always has a good future, a plan, and a hope for you.

I used to say that he was a God of the second chance. Now I think our God is much better than that. He is indeed the God of the second chance, but many of us already cashed that one in a while ago. Think about the Samaritan woman who had lived with so many different men (John 4). How many chances did she get? He is the God of amazing grace. We will never be able to count the number of chances we have gotten already or will get in the future. Now I have revised the "God of the second chance" to make it higher. He is the

God of the fifty-millionth chance, at least. His mercies are surely new *every* morning (Lamentations 3:23).

The only thing we need to do is to lean into him, or as old hymn says, "Trust and obey, for there's no better way to be happy in Jesus, but to trust and obey."

HE RESTORES WHAT IS LOST

There is a crazy story about the prophet Elisha and an iron ax head that floated on water, and the story foreshadows the events that made Jesus our redeemer. Here is a quick review of the story:

> One day the group of prophets came to Elisha and told him, "As you can see, this place where we meet with you is too small. Let's go down to the Jordan River, where there are plenty of logs. There we can build a new place for us to meet."
>
> "All right," he told them, "go ahead."
>
> "Please come with us," someone suggested.
>
> "I will," he said. So he [Elisha] went with them.
>
> When they arrived at the Jordan, they began cutting down trees. But as one of them was cutting a tree, his ax head fell into the river. "Oh, sir!" he cried. "It was a borrowed ax!"
>
> "Where did it fall?" the man of God asked. When he showed him the place, Elisha cut a stick and threw it into the water at that spot. Then the ax head floated to the surface. "Grab it," Elisha said. And the man reached out and grabbed it. (2 Kings 6:1–7 NLT)

Have you ever flown off the handle? Have you ever lost your

head? Have you ever lost your cutting edge? Have you ever been defeated right in the middle of your hard work? Have you ever forgotten until the mishap occurs that what you have lost was actually borrowed? Our lives are not our own, you know.

But the remedy for the lost ax head points to the remedy for every one of our losses. We find it at the end of the story. Elisha had the man point to the exact spot where the ax head had entered the water. (In the same way, God has us humble ourselves and identify honestly what has happened.) And then, wonder of wonders, there was hope after all! Elisha cut a stick from a tree. (The cross of Jesus is called the "tree.") He pulled back his arm and lobbed the stick right to that spot. A miracle occurred. The heavy ax head that had just sunk like a stone to the bottom of the river bobbed to the surface as if it were made of wood itself.

Hope! Miracles still happen. They never happen the way we think they should, but in the end, we are altogether grateful. With God, our valleys of trouble yield to doorways of hope every time.

I'm grateful to report that my cancer miracle happened at Zion. I had to endure some extremely difficult and expensive treatments. I also had some powerful prayer afterward. But as I sat in a small examination room, uncertain of what I would hear, my doctor matter-of-factly told me that my cancer was gone.

"What? Could you repeat that?"

"Your cancer is gone. It melted."

"You said the cancer *melted*?"

"Yes, it melted and is no longer in your body."

I left the treatment center stunned by what I had just heard. I found a small, quiet restaurant, and took out my phone to share the amazing news with my four children and a few close friends. Waves of gratitude and awe washed over me each time I said, "The cancer is gone. The doctor said it melted."

Miraculously, that cancer has never come back, and it is never going to come back again. I appeared before God in Zion (Psalm 84:5). I know beyond a shadow of doubt that I made it through the valley of the shadow of death. Iron can float, and cancer can melt away. I know. I am more than a survivor. I am an overcomer in Christ Jesus!

HEROINE OF HOPE: CORRIE TEN BOOM

Before World War II, Corrie ten Boom was a middle-aged Dutch woman who lived with her sister and widowed father. They were Christians active in charitable causes, and when the Nazis started persecuting the Jews in the Netherlands in 1940, the ten Boom family became part of the underground resistance; they built a secret hiding place behind the wall of a bedroom where they could hide small groups of the Jewish refugees with whom they were sharing their home secretly. They knew they were putting their own lives on the line to do so.

Four years later in the middle of the night, the dreaded knock came at the door. The German police arrested the entire family (although they did not discover the seven Jews who were hiding upstairs). Their father died within days after reaching the prison, but Corrie and her sister Betsie faced confinement under horrific conditions in a series of concentration camps, ending up in the infamous Ravensbrück in Germany. They held onto their faith and shared it with the other ragged, starving women confined in the barracks with them.

Betsie perished after ten months of punishing abuse, but

Corrie survived. After her release, she wrote a book called *The Hiding Place,* which became a movie of the same name. For the rest of her life, she traveled the world sharing one message: "There is no pit so deep that God's love is not deeper still." Her Valley of Achor had become a door of hope, and God turned her grievous losses into glory.

He will do the same for you and me. Isn't he a wonderful redeemer? Let your lost ax head float! Throw in the stick (a symbol of the cross of Christ). All things are possible!

PRAYER

Father, though I walk through the valley, I choose to trust in you! Turn my Valley of Achor into a door of hope. I believe that miracles still happen today. I believe that there is no pit so deep that your immense love cannot reach deeper. Restore me. Heal me. As I come before my Creator and Lord, turn my mourning into dancing. I believe you will guide me every step of the way, in your loving kindness. In Jesus's amazing name. Amen.

DISCOVERING HOPE TAKEAWAYS

Chapter 5
The Door of Hope

✦ God is your redeemer—he transforms trouble into victory and restores what was lost.

✦ Miracles still happen, although they never happen just the way you envisioned.

- Don't give up too soon. Keep moving forward.
- "Trust in the Lord with all your heart, and lean not on your own understanding; in all your ways acknowledge Him, and He shall direct your paths" (Proverbs 3:5–6 NKJV).
- Look for the door of hope just ahead and go through it.

CHAPTER 6

DUSTING OFF WEARINESS

Let us not lose heart in doing good,
for in due time we will reap if we do not grow weary.
GALATIANS 6:9 NASB

Have you ever grown weary in well-doing? Did you know that weariness is one of the most common enemies that attempts to get us in life's journey? In my own personal journey, I've been tempted to throw in the towel more than a time or two. These demonic forces can be very persistent at times. We have to realize that the powers of darkness do not let up once they temporarily knock us down.

I know I stated that a little differently because I'm acknowledging there are times in these stages that you do get knocked down. There are times you get hit on the head and you get knocked down, but what you've got to understand is that the enemy wants you to stay down. He's after you for the count. Once you do go down that downward spiral, he wants to keep you going deeper still. I'm telling you, the powers of darkness do not let up simply because they knocked us down.

But I also said "temporarily" because I know the Bible says in Proverbs 24:16 that the righteous will fall down and get back up. They'll get back up one more time, every time. That's the resiliency of God. It's the quickening power of the Holy Spirit. But we have to realize that we cannot wait for the powers of darkness to let up. In seasons like this, we have to rise up and shake off the dust of fatigue and weariness. We must learn to declare, "Thus far you shall come, but no further" (Job 38:11 NASB).

DOWN THE BURNOUT DRAIN

From that sense of negative emotions, we can easily give in to negative self-talk, mumbling to ourselves, griping, and complaining. We start to replay past negative experiences, and even start to sing the pity party songs of the past, like the famous hit from the 50s, "It's my party and I'll cry if I want to ... You would cry too if it happened to you." Or how about the song "Cry Me a River"? I know those are old examples, but these kinds of songs are a dime a dozen because that's where a lot of people live.

Well, guess what? Pity-parties don't go over well at any age, and whining isn't pretty at any age either. Like a two-year-old who's not getting his way, you can start to throw a tantrum, but as a grown adult, it turns into whining. Instead of being resilient and aglow with the Spirit, you become a frown-faced, old, wrinkled-up, shriveled-up person who lives in the past.

One specific way the powers of darkness like to knock us down is burnout. Yes, burnout can be a real and complex mixture of mental, emotional, physical, psychological, sexual, hormonal, chemical, and spiritual issues all wrapped up into one. It can affect your mood, your disposition, your energy levels, your sleep patterns, and ultimately your outlook on life. It becomes a ball of yarn, interwoven so that when you begin to pull on one thread, it feels as though the whole ball falls apart.

No matter what may have you feeling weary or knocked down, God has a remedy for every situation. We must learn to walk in healthy self-care, combining the disciplines of physical exercise, proper nutrition, relational community, edifying conversations, meditative prayer, and vibrant worship, among a few other things.

When I faced cancer in my body three times, I had to learn self-care on a completely new level. Stress will so often make us want to eat junk food for comfort when it is really just a way to poison ourselves. It can affect our sleep as well. All of these things affect our faith, hope, and love.

I cannot begin to tell you here all the things I learned about love or detoxing or proper nutrition while going through various alternative therapies and treatments for cancer. What I can tell you is, going on three times with cancer, today's world will try to nip the disease in the bud, but it doesn't destroy the root system that helped create the cultures that allowed the cancer to exist in the first place. A new friend of mine told me something really simple and rather quite profound: disease is anything that takes ease out of your life. Disease is a stress-filled life, but the real truth is that Jesus's yoke is easy and light!

Handling burnout properly is a big subject that I'm just touching briefly, but my main purpose here is to say that it isn't only rooted in the spiritual. It could be physical, it could be nutritional, it could be sleep patterns, or it could be that you're around the wrong community. It can be the need to cut off some relationships and build some new ones. All of that can be a part of burnout, and I encourage you to dig deeper into those other causes if that applies to you. Where I want to focus today is how to overcome the negativity from those seasons.

YOU GOTTA LOOK UP!

Whenever we face negativity, we need to remember a lesson from Psalm 121:1, "I will lift up my eyes to the mountains; from where shall my help come" (NASB). Take your chin off your chest! Remember: if you have to lift your eyes up, it means your chin is sitting on your chest and your eyes are looking on yourself.

This means, first, it is a decision to look up, but if you wait until your emotions feel like moving on, you never will. You will be a parked car in the cul-de-sac of yesterday. Second, what do you see when you look up? You see God, your source, and you connect to your place of strength. Third, what then do we do as we recognize him as our place of strength? We praise the Lord. We enter back into his gates with thanksgiving, into his courts with praise (Psalm 100:4). As we look up, we start to shift the atmosphere around us with praise. Praise is a sacrifice, and it will cost you something, but its rewards are worth it.

There's no wonder that the dear Lauren Daigle—one of today's most popular music artists, a dedicated soul, and Spirit-filled believer—has won Dove Awards, Grammys, and even three Billboard awards from her song and album *Look Up, Child*. It is one of the most relatable popular songs in recent years, and Lauren herself both penned and sang it. This song has brought hope to millions around the world. Here are the opening lyrics: "Where are You now, when darkness seems to win? Where are You now, when the world is crumbling?" The following lyric expresses how she hears the Lord say, "Look up, child."

Those lines are biblical and reminiscent of the psalmist's words. When our soul has cried out, *Where are you now?*, and when we're expressing our need for God to be not in our past but in our present, those lines are God the Father responding, *Look up, child.* In circumstances that would make us downcast, our Father calls us to look up and see that he is with us now.

A REAL ENEMY IS SET AGAINST YOU

We must realize that a real enemy is set against us. According to Ephesians 6:11–13, we are called to:

> Put on the full armor of God, so that you will be able to stand firm against the schemes of the devil. For our struggle is not against flesh and blood, but against the rulers, against the powers, against the world forces of this darkness, against the spiritual forces of wickedness in the heavenly places. Therefore, take up the full armor of God, so that you will be able to resist in the evil day, and having done everything, to stand firm. (NASB)

Another great passage to give us proper biblical understanding that a real enemy is set against us is 2 Corinthians 10:3–6:

> For though we walk in the flesh, we do not war according to the flesh, for the weapons of our warfare are not of the flesh, but divinely powerful for the destruction of fortresses. We are destroying speculations and every lofty thing raised up against the knowledge of God, and we are taking every thought captive to the obedience of Christ, and we

are ready to punish all disobedience, whenever your obedience is complete. (NASB)

Notice, it does say we wage war, we just do not wage war the way the world does. In fact, we wage war in many ways, and one of the ways we do is to take every thought captive. We must captivate all those negative thoughts, all those weary thoughts, all those thoughts that want to stay down and quit, and we must force them into obedience to Christ.

This is fascinating to me. This passage gives the warrior, you and me, the right to even inflict punishment—"and we are ready to punish all disobedience, whenever your obedience is complete." Now, I've done thorough teachings on these subjects in my book *Deliverance from Darkness*. I just am giving you some biblical reference here to show a real enemy exists.

A look at Daniel 7:25 helps us understand one of the ways this very real enemy works against us. The first half of the verse says, "He will speak out against the Most High and wear down the saints of the Highest One" (NASB). I thoroughly cover this area in my book *The Discerner*, as I teach there about different demonic spirits, their personage, and how they operate, but I will tell you here, this is a spirit of antichrist. He acts in this manner: he comes against believers in an attempt to *wear them down.*

Look at that again; see what it says. One primary purpose of the devil or the spirit of the antichrist is to come against the saints—believers like you and me—and he will attempt to wear you down. We must know the enemy's schemes and learn to rise above them and take a stand. Or how about a promise from Isaiah 40:28–31:

Do you not know? Have you not heard? The Ever-
lasting God, the Lord, the Creator of the ends of the

earth does not become weary or tired. His under-standing is inscrutable. He gives strength to the weary, and to him who lacks might He increases power. Though youths grow weary and tired, and vigorous young men stumble badly, yet those who wait for the Lord will gain new strength; they will mount up with wings like eagles, they will run and not get tired, they will walk and not become weary. (NASB)

Did you see? The Lord, the Creator, does not become weary or tired. This is dusting off fatigue and weariness on an entirely new level. He simply doesn't become worn out, but we must shake it off. I'm telling you that you must do it. *You* must shake off the weari-ness. Other people can pray for you and help dust you off, but you have to shake it off for it to stay off. Yes, times will come when you have gone as far as you can on the strength you have, but when you minister to the Lord, you will gain new strength.

God promises a turnaround for everything the enemy tries to throw at us. There is a cure for burnout. There is a remedy in the Holy Spirit for every condition of fatigue, weariness, and mental and emotional depletion. We must learn to continue to abide in him and in the power of his Word.

HANDLING THE ISSUES OF GUILT

There's another issue that's interrelated here with weariness and fatigue, and it's an issue called guilt. There are three categories of guilt—true guilt, exaggerated guilt, and false guilt—and we have to deal with each one of these.

True guilt is healthy and comes because our hand was caught

in the cookie jar, proverbially speaking, and it wasn't supposed to be there. Properly responding to true guilt means that, as believers, we welcome the convicting work of the Holy Spirit in our lives. We must yield to this cleansing and sanctifying grace of God. It is a good thing to come under conviction. You cannot rebuke away real guilt or say to it, *Be gone.* That isn't the way it works. The removal of guilt requires an honest, transparent relationship with God where you're walking in the light, the only place where cleansing occurs. We have to bring true guilt to God and ask Jesus to cleanse us with his blood, ask God to forgive us, and apply the washing of the water of the Word to our soul.

There's also exaggerated guilt. Many believers deal with this, and they're not aware it even exists. At times, our emotions are clouded with distorted views of reality. The enemy also attempts to expand true guilt by putting a magnifying glass up to our shortcomings and faults. That's the tricky thing about exaggerated guilt: it's based on wrongs we actually did. To get rid of the exaggerated guilt, first ask the Holy Spirit for his conviction and the truth. This will help you discern what is the true guilt. Deal with that root guilt then do it no longer. Once you clean up the true mess, nothing remains for the enemy to magnify. When you know you stand clean and forgiven before God, you have to tell the little foxes, *Be gone.* Don't bother with exaggerated guilt a moment longer than necessary, but instead, stand in the truth.

This will require us at times to speak to our own emotions. King David gives us a great example in this, declaring, "Why, my soul, are you downcast?" (Psalm 43:5 NIV). At times, you have to talk to those places of trauma, stored memories, unhealed emotions, or guilt. We have to be like a priest in the Old Testament, lay-ing his hands on the scapegoat, naming the sins, and then telling it to be gone.

Just as there are real guilt and exaggerated guilt, there is also flat-out it's-not-true, it's-made-up, it's-fabricated, it's-fake-news false guilt. In this case, the guilty feelings in one's thought patterns and emotions may not be rooted in actual reality. It could be a case of faulty perception caused by an open door of rejection, insecurity, or trauma. Responding properly to false guilt requires learning our true identity because this guilt is a fantasy; it's not true. You didn't do it, and even if you did, you've already confessed it, and God has forgiven you, cleansed you, and thrown it into the sea of forgetfulness. If you keep bringing it up, he isn't going to remember.

Our acceptance is by grace. It's by love. It's by what Jesus has already done; we can't earn it. Our salvation is through Jesus, but there are times we've got to take that same realm of grace and apply it to other areas of our emotions, soul, or memories. This requires thoroughly learning our identity in Christ Jesus, not performance-based acceptance.

Ultimately the cure for all issues of guilt is the same—the sacrificial Lamb of God who was slain for our sinful condition. Thank God for the blood of the Lamb!

SHAKE IT OFF

People often say, "Shame on you," and I want to draw a line on that issue. Parents, please do not say these words to your children. If you have, just repent. Ask God to forgive you, and then forgive yourself. Yes, forgive yourself; we are often harder on ourselves than even the devil is. But we cannot allow ourselves to say, "Shame on." In fact, do the opposite: "Shame off."

There's a difference between conviction with guilt and condemnation through shame. They don't feel the same. They do initially, and that's why we buy it. Guilt lasts for a while, but the convicting, cleansing work of the blood of Jesus removes it. Shame is flypaper, and it sticks around. When people say, "Shame on you," it's not a proper perspective at all; it is actually a damaging and ungodly belief. Shame is a false weight that causes a person to cower, back off, and go into hiding, morbid introspection, and condemnation. The Holy Spirit convicts in order to heal and deliver, but the devil condemns to release oppression and suppression. It's not, "Shame on you;" it should be, "Shame off, in the name and the blood of Jesus."

I look at Hebrews 12:1 to learn about this: "Therefore, since we have so great a cloud of witnesses surrounding us, let us also lay aside every encumbrance and the sin which so easily entangles us, and let us run with endurance the race that is set before us" (NASB).

Let me tell you the first thing I see in this verse that helps raise me out of weariness and discouragement. I see here that, in a truly wonderful way, I'm one day closer to being reunited with my parents, my grandparents, and my wife. I'm also one day closer to a miracle. I'm one day closer to fullness of joy, one day closer to the fruits of love, peace, patience, kindness, and greater self-control being more predominant in my life.

In the meantime, I also see that I must run with endurance, that life is not a short sprint. Finally, I see the command to get free from the entanglements of the world that hinder me and my progress. We must lay aside these things, even cast them off. There is no room for shame to hinder us any longer. Dust yourself off. Hebrews 9:13–14 is also invaluable to us here:

> For if the blood of goats and bulls and the ashes of a heifer sprinkling those who have been defiled sanctify for the cleansing of the flesh, how much more will the blood of Christ, who through the eternal Spirit offered Himself without blemish to God, cleanse your conscience from dead works to serve the living God? (NASB)

See the phrase, "Cleanse your conscience from dead works to serve the living God." Our conscience has to get cleansed, and not just from evil works but also from dead works. Those can even be religious works done in a wrong motive. If it's not alive, it's dead, and the Bible says that we can get cleansed from that death. We can get cleansed from that heaviness. We can get cleansed where there is true light in our soul, a true light in our eyes, so that our countenance has been lifted up. The remedy is ever the same.

According to Leviticus 5, there is a guilt offering that the priest offers up before the Lord on behalf of the people, and Jesus is the sacrificial Lamb that was slain for sin. We know the power and the benefits of the blood of the Lamb, Jesus Christ. Over the years I have often taught about the work of the cross of Jesus Christ. The Word of God declares from cover to cover, "By the blood I am forgiven, cleansed, redeemed, justified, sanctified, have peace, have access to the throne of almighty God."

The old gospel song is correct: "What can wash away my sin?" We might even adapt it for the purposes of this chapter to "What can wash away my guilt?" But the answer is ever the same: "Nothing but the blood of Jesus." Let the truth of these words wash over you, "Oh, precious is the flow that makes me white as snow.

No other fount I know, nothing but the blood of Jesus," because there really is power in the blood of Jesus.

HERO OF HOPE: JAMES MALONEY

Now I want to introduce you to another one of my friends who I consider a hero of faith, hope, and love: none other than Dr. James Maloney. He's a friend, and we are peers, though I feel very humbled and honored that this man would consider me a peer or a friend. He is really in God's hall of fame of Heroes of Hope. He's known as a healing evangelist, doing signs, wonders, and miracles through a rather amazing gift of faith. He's also a seer prophet. I wrote *The Seer*, but he wrote *Panoramic Seer*.

James Maloney has one of the most heart-wrenching testimonies of a hero of hope that I know. From a background of utter abandonment and abuse, faith has transformed James into a deliverer of men. James's mother was married, but while her husband was in prison, she became pregnant with James by another man. When her husband came home from prison and found his wife pregnant when he had not been with her, that didn't set up a good scene. This man abused James because he was not actually his.

That marriage ended in divorce, and his mother married a second time, but the patterns didn't necessarily get better. In fact, they got worse because as a child, James was abandoned to live in a little, dark closet, shut off from outside communications and nurture. His mother was so poor that she hid him in the closet, and she'd only open the door to give him bites of food to eat. At times, his mother hid him to protect him from the combative destruction of her second husband. He lived in that dark place for three years. He was beaten multiple times so severely that his head was literally caved in in some places. From that severe crushing, James received a call to take God's healing power with a gift of faith and the workings of miracles to the world.

I've heard some testify that James walks in the greatest gift of faith of anyone they know in this generation. Having ministered with him, I have heard James state that he doesn't move in gifts of healing or working of miracles, but he moves in a gift of faith. When someone goes to him, it's the gift of faith that kicks in. He moves into the seer realm and, because of what he went through, often he will see traumas that lead later to sicknesses and diseases, helping him address the root issue and bring lasting healing. Through God, James has overcome much, and now his lifestyle as a perpetual overcomer leads to him moving in demonstrative realms of the power of God.

In recent years, James received a terrible diagnosis. The physical abuse he received as child resulted in broken fragments of bone in his face, producing a severe case of squamous cell carcinoma, SCC, that resulted in extraordinarily extreme pain, loss of sight, brain tumors, and much more. He ended up having to have multiple reconstructive surgeries on his head and face. To this day, he has to wear sunglasses because his eyes are still being restored from the brain tumors. In the midst of this, James could just ask, *Why, why, why?* but God showed him an end result of his life, and he knows that he's now entering stage four of this healing power gift that's on his life.

I pray that he will have more triumph over the powers of darkness in these next years than all of it put together because he still faces difficulty, he still is dealing with anguish and pain, but he is being restored. Yet even while he fights his own battles, he keeps his hand on the plow. James is determined to be a walking dead man who is dead to self and alive in Christ.

That's the truth because faith, hope, and love will have the final say. Through it all, deeper understanding of the compassion of God has flooded into this man's life, combined with the revelation of the love of God in four dimensions. While still a work in progress, James is walking in greater faith, hope, and love and is back ministering on the international stage.

James is a true hope ambassador of the Lord Jesus Christ, operating in the gift of faith where all things are possible, even if you suffered severe abuse in your childhood. This is a small reason why I also nominate Dr. James Maloney into my Hall of Heroes of Faith, Hope, and Love.

PRAYER

*Father, by the grace you supply, I choose
to shake off the dust of fatigue and weariness.
I choose to keep my hand on the plow and
not look back. Rather, I determine to look up,
knowing that you are my help and my strength
in times of trouble. I present myself to you to
be cleansed in the blood of Jesus from the
weight of shame and guilt, and I declare that in
you I live and breathe and have my very being.
In Jesus's name we shake it off. We dust off
weariness and fatigue, for Jesus Christ's sake.
Amen and amen.*

DISCOVERING HOPE TAKEAWAYS

Chapter 6
Dusting Off Weariness

✦ We have a real enemy. We must recognize his attack, working to wear us down and burn us out. Then, once you recognize his attack, declare in Jesus's name, "Thus far but no further!"

✦ Remember the three types of guilt: true guilt, exaggerated guilt, and false guilt. Whenever you feel guilty, don't sit in it; process it right away!

• Repent of anything you did deserving of true guilt.

• Recognize any guilt that is exaggerated or false and shake it off!

• Forgive yourself, forgive others, and move forward under the blood of the Lamb.

CHAPTER 7

A HEART THAT SINGS

Be strong and let your heart take courage,
all you who hope in the Lord.
PSALM 31:24 NASB

It was time for me to trade in my old PT Cruiser for something new, so I went to visit a car dealership. At the door, a gentleman met me with a smile, and we talked about what I wanted to look at. Then after a while, we went into his office and sat down together. I might have said something about losing my wife to cancer; I don't really remember. But out of the blue, the car dealer said, "I am going to give you a book. The name of it is *Life Between Sundays.*"

I thanked him and took it home with me. As it turns out, a prominent, local African-American preacher named Joseph W. Walker III, who pastors one of the largest churches in the greater metropolitan Nashville area, had written the book. I did not know him personally, but after reading his book, I decided that I wanted to meet him. He, too, had lost his wife to cancer, and I wanted to hear the rest of his story.

I had a mutual friend introduce us, and I went over to his church to meet him. Guess what the name of his church is? Mount Zion. That caught my attention, for sure. Since his wife's death, he had worked through his deep valley of grief, written several more books, and pastored his church, which had continued to grow and flourish. He had also remarried and had welcomed his first child into the world. We compared notes. He and his wife are very well educated, clearly on the growing edge in their careers and ministry. But our heart-issues are the same, and we share the same Jesus. As I stood up to leave, we blessed each other.

Then he turned to me and added, "You need to know this. The heart is the most amazing organ in the entire body. It has many chambers. I will always have a special chamber in my heart for my first love, my first wife. But I was surprised when another door opened up in my heart, and I saw that I had a chamber for my second wife as well. My heart is bigger than it used to be. Now it is full."

I walked out that day knowing that I had just heard a much-needed word (in Zion!). I thought about what he had said about his heart, and it made me consider my own heart. I had been carrying my half-dead heart around for too long. Maybe it was time to speak life to it. I was not thinking about a new wife, but maybe I needed to get some special heart-attention from the One who created it and who had kept it beating all the way through the valley of the shadow of death.

WATCHING OVER YOUR HEART

I knew the Lord would be more than willing to help me. I had plenty of verses to go on. For example, "The eyes of the Lord move to and fro throughout the earth that He may strongly support those whose heart is completely His" (2 Chronicles 16:9 NASB). I may have thought that my heart no longer held anything but despair, but nevertheless it was "completely His." In fact, my heart was more completely his than ever because of how much I had been forced to rely on his love and strength and wisdom. His heart truly wanted to "strongly support" mine? How awesome to think about that!

Jesus said, "You shall love the Lord your God with all your heart, with all your soul, and with all your mind" (Matthew 22:37 NKJV). How could I rev up my heart again in order to love him wholly? In order to love God with every fiber of my being, I was going to have to figure out how to get it beating stronger than ever. I inaugurated a new goal: to end this race better than I started it. I decided that after I go home to God, I want people to say, "James Goll loved God, and he taught other people how to love him too."

The state of my heart was crucial to the next steps I would take. I would have to guard it and look after its welfare, following the advice of the proverb: "Watch over your heart with all diligence, for from it flow the springs [issues] of life" (Proverbs 4:23 NASB). To resuscitate it fully, I would have to learn how to speak life to it.

FINDING MY BEARINGS

Any time of trials and transition is enormously hard on your heart and soul and might even spill over to affect your body also. Even if you try to keep loving God and others as well as you used to, you just might not have as much of a reservoir to work from as before. Even when things settle down a little, you may remain exhausted from grieving and adjusting to your new reality. You know you are still on a journey, but you do not find it easy to get your bearings.

Finding your bearings has to become part of the journey, or

you will just go in circles. You have to ask yourself some basic questions, such as: *Who am I? What do my roots tell me about myself? What do I love to do? What brings me life?*

Who am I? This is easy to answer, right? Well, not when you are still reassembling your identity after a major trauma or loss. I had been married to the same person for over half my life, and my identity to a large degree revolved around being her husband. Now I was a grieving widower. Still, I was a father, right? Yet my kids were all leaving the nest to make marriages and families of their own. It would have been a time of major readjustment for me even without the cancer and Michal Ann's death. I was still in full-time vocational ministry. I could teach. I still prayed; I was an active intercessor. I kept thinking about it.

What do my roots tell me about myself? To find by bearings, I had to reevaluate my personal history. I decided to look back at my childhood and to revive some good memories. For example, I recalled the way I would help my dad, who was the treasurer of our little Methodist church for several years, count the Sunday offering after church. We would bring the offering home, and after lunch we would count the money on the turquoise kitchen table, this being the fifties. My dad would pour out the offering, and a lot of it was coins because people who do not have much money tend to put quarters, dimes, nickels, and even pennies in the offering plate. Before we counted the money, we would sort out every wheat penny, buffalo nickel, and Mercury dime because the government wasn't issuing any of those coins anymore, and Dad collected them.

He would pay back the offering with newer coins, of course, and put the day's finds aside in his growing coin collection. Many years later when my father died, my sisters and I inherited his coin collection. At that point, I resumed my interest, and I began to create my own collection, which includes samples of money from many of the countries I have visited in the course of my ministry. Someday I will pass on my father's old coin collection and my own distinct collection to my own children.

So besides being a spiritual leader and father, I am a novice coin-collector. Somehow recognizing that helps me find my bearings a little bit more. I love to work on that collection, although I don't suppose I was born to be a coin collector. I was, however, born to sing.

BORN TO SING

When I asked myself, *What do I love to do?* one of my first answers was *I love to sing.* I have been singing since at least the age of three, and in high school I won awards for singing as other young guys might win awards for basketball or some other sport. I didn't sing in order to win prizes; I sang because it was my life. I would go on walks down the railroad tracks, and I would sing Sunday school songs and hymns from the brownish-red Cokesbury hymnal. I would sing anything I heard. I would sing with the radio. I would sing with Lawrence Welk. I would sing everywhere I went! I grew up being known as a singer.

I kept on singing after I grew up and got married. (Somebody gave me a T-shirt that reads, "I sing real loud.") I would sing when I was happy, and I would sing when I was sad. I would sing in the shower and sing in the car. I would sing during corporate worship, and I would sing in the middle of my own sermons. It didn't matter if I was having a "bad voice or good voice" day—I would just sing anyway.

But in the midst of my pain, lately I discovered that had not been singing much at all. Once I put my finger on the fact that I was *born* to sing, I figured out that one of the best keys for unlocking my somewhat beat-up heart would be *telling my heart to sing again.* I would sing life back into it.

I think that is something anyone could do, even those who cannot sing a note. Even if you don't use outright singing to do it, at least you could *speak* to your heart to revive it. Tell your heart the truth. Tell your heart who is on the throne. Tell your heart about God's faithfulness and goodness and how much the Shepherd cares. Ask yourself, *What brings me life?* Look back across the years to find precious memories and helpful clues about what works for you. Read the Bible as if God wrote it to you personally, rereading the parts that speak most to you. To experience the hidden power of praise and singing, start with Psalms 148, 149, and 150. Tell your heart to start singing!

I started singing again. Now I sing my pain away most every day. I sing day and night. I sing in every hotel room I go into. I sing in my kitchen. I sing outside when I take a walk. I sing by myself, and I sing with others. I recently sang crooner songs in a marble lobby of a five-star hotel in Taipei, Taiwan, with a classical pianist. People started coming up to take videos thinking I was an internationally famous singer; after all, I do reside in Nashville! But a lot of the time I sing the old hymns I love. Their lyrics bring stability to my soul:

> "My hope is built on nothing less than Jesus's blood and righteousness. I dare not trust the sweetest frame, but wholly lean on Jesus's name. On Christ the solid rock I stand; all other ground is sinking sand … When he shall come with trumpet

sound, oh may I then in him be found, dressed in his righteousness alone, faultless to stand before the throne."

Hidden within the lyrics and melodies, the power of praise and worship builds up my heart and orients me in the right direction. It sometimes takes a moment to overcome feeling shut down, too sad, and too tired to breathe out a note of a song, but once I make the effort, I am so glad I am alive and held in God's capable hands.

A RENEWED CALLING

This joy in rediscovering singing led me on a path that was both surprising and fulfilling. The Holy Spirit dropped in my heart the call to record inspirational music that the world knew and loved. So I practiced four pieces of music for six months and designed my own distinct arrangements of them. I then did an audition before a well-known Grammy and Dove award producer, whom I did not even qualify to be in the room with.

The audition went so-so until I performed the last piece of music. That morning the Holy Spirit told me in a dream that I did not know how to sing the song properly and to sing it with a half voice and a softer tone. I said to the Lord, *I do not know how to do that! I have never sung that way in my lifetime. I sing BIG!* Nonetheless, the Lord won out. I shifted the last piece of music into a style and tone that I was not familiar with and then the producer stated, "That is what we are looking for!" God knows, and God knew I did not know. His ways are best!

For the following two years, I spent scores of hours taking professional vocal lessons and relearning how to sing. I knew my twenty-something-year-old voice, but I did not know my sixty-five-year-old voice. I had to learn new skills. It not only gave me some-thing to offer to the world, but the journey also made me a more relatable man. I chose as my theme song a piece of music from the 1940s musical Carrousel, "You'll Never Walk Alone." Thus, the title of the recording is *Never Alone*[3]. It tells my life's journey in song and invites others to tell their hearts to sing again. This has been a dream come true for me to return to my roots and rediscover hope for life. I learned more in the process of recording music than I had learned in the last thirty years in any field of study. I learned the ins and outs of the music industry, which has hopefully made me more connectable to the city where I live: Music City, U.S.A. But I am not the only one who has a song to sing. We are each born to release the sounds of life.

I have a special song to sing with my life, and so do you. Not only do we need to tell our hearts to sing again, we need to hear (and learn) each other's songs. One story can best explain this idea, which, although it may be folklore, I want to share here:

TEACH ME YOUR SONG

In the northern parts of Africa, there is a semi-nomadic tribe that counts the birthday of a child not from the day of birth or even the day of conception but the day the mother first decides to have the child.

When a woman decides to have a child, she goes off and sits under a tree by herself, and she listens until she can hear the song of the child that wants to come. After she has heard the song of this child, she comes back to the man who will be the child's father and teaches him the song. Then, when they make love to

---

3   *Never Alone* is available on all of today's musical digital platforms and hard copy CD from my ministry resource center at jamesgoll.com.

physically conceive the child, they sing the song of the child as a way to invite the child.

When she becomes pregnant, the mother teaches that child's song to the midwives and the old women of the village, so when the child is born, the old women and the people around her sing the child's song to welcome it. As the child grows up, the other villagers learn the child's song. If the child falls or gets hurt, someone picks the child up and sings that child's song to him or her. If the child does something wonderful or goes through the rites of puberty, then the people of the village sing his or her song to show honor.

In the tribe, there is one other occasion when they will sing the child's song: when the person does something hurtful and wrong. They take the person to the center of town and the entire tribe comes and surrounds him or her. They sing the person's birth song and then for two days they tell the man or woman every *good* thing he or she has ever done.

The tribe believes that every human being comes into the world as good—desiring safety, love, peace, and happiness, but sometimes in the pursuit of those ideals, people make mistakes. The community sees misdeeds as a cry for help. They band together for the sake of their fellow tribesperson to reconnect the person with his or her true nature and to remind the person who he or she really is until the person fully remembers the truth: *I am good.* They view correction for antisocial behavior not as a punishment but as love and remembrance of identity. For when you recognize your own song, you have no desire or need to do anything that would hurt another. That sounds to me like a restoration of hope.

So a person's song is the theme of his or her life. In marriage, the husband's and wife's songs are sung together. Finally, when the person is lying in his bed and ready to die, all the villagers who know the song come and sing that person's song for the last time.

You may not have grown up in an African tribe that sings your song to you at crucial life transitions, but your life is always reminding you when you are in tune with yourself and when you are not. You feel good when your actions match your song, and you feel awful when they do not. When you lose your bearings, you lose your song for a time. When you get back in touch with who you are, you rediscover your song. It will not be enough to sing your song to yourself. Sometimes you need to sing your song for me and teach it to me. We are called to live our lives in community, and we need to learn each other's songs.

As it happens, I made up songs for each of our four kids, and I used to sing to them every night when I was home at their bedtime. I remember my oldest son's the best. Here is the ending of it: "I like to dream about butterflies, I like to dream about stars in the sky, and I like to dream about you-hoo. I like to dream about you-hoo, and I like to dream about you. Bumpty-bump." Then I would tickle him, and he would laugh. How sweet it has been to take that lullaby from years ago and adapt it into a musical style that fit right into the closing section of my "Never Alone" recording. Today my grandkids sing Grampa's song, "I Like to Dream," as though it were written for them, and maybe it was!

WHAT IS GOD SINGING OVER YOU?

I believe that God has a song for us to sing over each other, over whole families, over cities, and over nations. Sometimes when I go to a city to minister, I ask God, *What song are you singing over this city?* I ask him to tune the ear of my heart to heaven so that maybe I can hear a little bit of what heaven is singing there.

God himself is the "singing God," you know: "The Lord your God is with you, the Mighty Warrior who saves. He will take great delight in you; in his love he will no longer rebuke you, but will rejoice over you with singing" (Zephaniah 3:17 NIV). What is God singing over you? I can tell you that he is singing an anthem of hope. He is singing, *I love you and I have a plan for you. I have a great future for you. I have you on my mind and in my heart. I am working everything together for you.*

HERO OF HOPE: DANNY GOKEY

This next hero of hope is a giant of a singer. He used to be a church music director in Milwaukee, Wisconsin, and now he is a professional singer in Nashville. He and I attend church and Bible study together, and I have had the pleasure of getting to know him. You may have heard his name because of his music or because of his book *Hope in Front of Me: Find Purpose in Your Darkest Moments.* A few years ago, he competed on *American Idol* (when the show was still in its prime) and came in third place.

His *American Idol* performance took place very soon after his young wife, Sophia, had died during heart surgery. So the fact that he stayed in the running as long as he did was amazing to him. He was still in grief and, as he puts it, "Ten months before, I stood at my wife's casket, and I wanted to die along with her."

Yet he refused to let his hope-defeating circumstances define his life. He chose to believe that God had a bigger plan for his life. He wrote some more songs. He went on tour. He started a charitable foundation in the Nashville area called Sophie's Heart, which helps to meet the needs of children and families. What could have been a dead end became a detour and a new beginning. He told his heart to sing again.

Hope is big for Danny, and he is helping make it big with me. He did not get bitter. Even when he was emotionally, spiritually, and physically spent, he kept on trusting God. He kept following the thread of hope that connected him with the eternal life source; it was his lifeline. Hope reminded him that life exists beyond what we can see, hear, taste, smell, or touch. Hope was always just in front of him, and it still is. Danny released a new album to go alongside his book, and the title song is, of course, "Hope in Front of Me." In this season of his life, Danny is the headliner performer for the Hope Encounter tour.

Eventually he married a beautiful prayer warrior named Leyicet, and they now have four adorable children together. He has won multiple awards with his music of hope and is recognized as one of the top male singers today. Danny is actually about the same age as my oldest son, but this dear man lives his songs and exemplifies the message of this book. So, Danny Gokey is a hero of hope for me. We need heroes of hope in all walks of life. Are you building your own Hall of Heroes?

PRAYER

Father, I believe that all of creation is a painting of your beauty and majesty. I believe that you sing over your creation—including me. I believe that the heart is an amazing organ and that out of it flow the springs and issues of life. My heart needs to be revived. I want to tell it to sing again. I speak life to my heart, and I declare, "Hope is standing right in front of me," because you are right in front of me, even right inside my heart. For the glory of God in Jesus's name. Amen.

DISCOVERING HOPE TAKEAWAYS

Chapter 7
A Heart that Sings

✦ Jesus said, "You shall love the Lord your God with all your heart, with all your soul, and with all your mind" (Matthew 22:37 NKJV). A hopeless heart cannot do this. Tell your heart what to do.

✦ Get your bearings by reviewing your personal history and remembering what you love to do.

✦ Believe that God has a hope and a future for you.

✦ Declare to your own heart: *Hope is standing in front of me.*

CHAPTER 8

LET GOD PUT A DREAM IN YOUR HEART

In hope against hope he believed, so that he [Abraham] might become a
father of many nations according to that which had been spoken,
"so shall your descendants be."
ROMANS 4:18 NASB

"God gave me another dream!" seventeen-year-old Joseph exclaimed to his eleven brothers as they gathered in the early morning light before heading out to their day's tasks. "Let me tell you about it."

The brothers glowered at their youngest brother. Already they disliked him more than ever. "This egotistical kid is getting on my nerves," muttered Levi. The men shifted restlessly as Joseph told them some farfetched dream about eleven stars, along with the sun and moon, bowing down before him reverentially. *It sounds like he thinks he's not only our father's favorite son, but God's favorite too. Just last week he had that other dream about sheaves of grain bowing to him.* For the most part, the older brothers kept their resentful thoughts hidden, but they began to consider ways to shut up young Joseph for good.

By the end of the month they had eliminated him from the family—or so they thought—and now his arrogance would never trouble them again. *This is what happens to self-aggrandizing dreamers,* they reflected bitterly as they drove the family's flocks home from Shechem. Reuben carried Joseph's bloody coat to their father Jacob, along with the bad news about his apparent demise from an attack of a wild beast.

Many people have retold the story of the dreamer Joseph (you can review it by reading chapters 37–43 of the book of Genesis). God-inspired dreams determined the direction for Joseph's entire life. He went from pit to pinnacle, daring to trust that God was in charge of every dream-determined decision.

Those first two dreams were God's way of showing him that someday, incredible as it might seem, he would be honored as if he were a patriarch or a pharaoh. His brothers' simmering resentment soon tried to put the lie to such pretentious-sounding predictions when they ganged up on Joseph far from home and threw him into a deep pit. Preparing a lie to tell their father about what had happened, they sold their brother as a slave to a passing caravan of merchants, who took Joseph even farther from home to Egypt, selling him into service in Potiphar's household, the captain of Pharaoh's guard.

Joseph proved to be such a capable and trustworthy servant that the pharaoh promoted him to his personal assistant. He was also too good-looking for Potiphar's wife to resist, and when the righteous young Hebrew spurned her seductive advances, she had him thrown into the dungeon with no promise of parole.

While confined in the Egyptian prison, Joseph put his dream-interpretation skills to good use, making something of a reputation for himself. In due time, the pharaoh himself had a portentous dream for which he urgently needed an interpreter, and he summoned Joseph. His explicit and accurate interpretation won him not only his freedom from prison but also a new, high-level assignment in the royal household. As second in command, he now managed the resources of the nation of Egypt, preparing for the famine that the pharaoh's dream had predicted. As the crops began to fail in the seventh year and famine ensued, Joseph was ready; Egypt would be saved.

It had been at least fifteen years since Joseph's brothers threw him into the pit near Shechem. Once the famine spread as far as Canaan, where they still lived with their father, it forced the brothers to travel to prosperous Egypt, where they had heard they could obtain food. To whom must they apply for relief? Unbeknownst to them, the Egyptian official to whom they were bowing (like sheaves of grain!) was none other than their maligned brother, Joseph.

Joseph knew who they were. Was he vengeful as he looked down at the tops of their bowed heads? No, he saw the fulfillment of his dream. Fifteen long and eventful years had passed, but Joseph had not let his dream die. He couldn't. His dream had taken hold of him. Now he could see what God had intended all along. Through everything that had happened, God was going to use him to continue the legacy of his family line until the fulfillment of more dreams. Joseph said to his brothers: "As for you, you meant to harm me, but God intended it for a good purpose, so he could preserve the lives of many people, as you can see this day" (Genesis 50:20 NET).

God intentionally planted Joseph's dreams and, knowing the evil hearts of men, had once again made sure that malicious decisions and disastrous events would work together to bring a miraculous outcome with blessed eternal consequences.

LET GOD PUT DESIRE IN YOUR HEART

The Jewish people are still reaping the blessings of Joseph's dreams today, and so are we, as we learn from his story how God works. And God is still giving dreams to his people, including you and me. He is still making it possible for us to move into the future with hope. The last thing he wants is for us to live in the past, sorrowing over our yesterdays.

God never lives in the past, and he wants to bring you into the future he has in mind. He wants to put his desires into your heart. He wants to give you his dreams for your life. Even if you feel that adversity has deadened your heart to the point that it can no longer receive a thing, be assured that your Father can fix that too. Remember the idea I presented in the previous chapter: God can open up another chamber in your heart. He wants to do that for you. He can increase the capacity of your heart. God is ready to resuscitate your dead heart and plant seeds of hope in it.

I have a friend who had to have quadruple bypass surgery. Three of his arteries were over 90 percent obstructed, and he could have died of a heart attack at any moment. Thanks to the surgery, his life has been preserved and extended, and we call him "the man with the iron heart" because his heart used to have to beat so hard to pump blood through those obstructed arteries that it became stronger than the average heart. I see a parable here.

God knows what he's doing when he allows us to go through

a major time of difficulty. Among other things, he intends to make our hearts and faith much stronger. He takes us out of our dark pit of suffering so that we can proceed with the extended life he has planned for us, although we may not be able to see the whole picture until later.

Just as my friend did not have to operate on himself, so all you need to do in order to cooperate with God is to present yourself to him. That's all. Today, this dear man, Mark Roye, carries on the ministry that my late wife started, Compassion Acts. It makes possible another divine injection of hope, reaching across the world.

You don't have to figure out everything ahead of time. You don't have to get your act together to prove how worthy you are of God's attention. You only need to daringly dream the dream that he wants to give you. Present yourself to him. *Here I am, Lord.* Open your heart to him, even though it seems as if traumatic events have crushed it.

Now, you might need to tell your heart that it's okay to dream again. I had to give my heart permission to have desires and longings again. For the past few years, I have been on a very intentional journey of what brings life to me: discovering hope. After having traveled the world and visited people in high places and then spending time on the backside of the desert, I felt I needed to explore my unfulfilled dreams. I asked myself, *Do I still have wishes, hopes, desires that I long to see transpire before the end of my life? What do I think about establishing a lineage and a legacy?*

It has taken me time to realize that I am not only fighting to stay alive just for the sake of my kids, although that is quite noble. I have made a deep internal decision that it is not enough for me to be a survivor of cancer and then just sit on the sidelines of life wearing a t-shirt that says, "Been There, Done That!" I have tilled the soil of my heart and called forth the Word of God (like Jeremiah of old) to be a hammer that will shatter any hard places that remain.

Today, I am exploding with new ideas. Bucket list? I don't have one! But I am now preparing to start my own business called GOLL Ideation, including consulting, leadership development, and more. I am even a business partner with two other men in a new restaurant chain and a tax business. I was once half dead, but I am coming back to life! I launched other new ministry ventures, like the *God Encounters Today* podcast, and I've recorded video devotions that air on GOD TV. The new me is even peering into men's fashion and design. I have a desire in my heart to become a Renaissance man who can make an impact on all of the cultural "mountains" with explosive Kingdom-of-Light displays!

"But," you say, "my heart is worn out." So make it a point to confess your faith in God's faithfulness. Be quick to obey when the Holy Spirit nudges you into action. Watch for signs of new life in your heart, and be ready to perceive new connections between your past, present, and future. You can change Psalm 20:4–5 into a prayer for yourself: *Lord, grant me the desires of my heart, which only you could have put there. Fulfill all of your wishes for me, so that everyone around me will sing for joy over your victory in my life. Lord of my life, hear my heartfelt prayers.*

Thirty years ago, I was deeply moved by a book called *Don't Waste Your Sorrows* by Paul Billheimer, who did not go into full-time vocational ministry until he retired. This rocked my world because he did not discover what God created him for until he was sixty-five years old! He showed me that you are never too old to discover fresh purpose and meaning in life. He showed me what it looks like when God puts a dream into your heart. I never knew how much I would need the message of that simple book until three decades later, but God knew. Instead of wasting your sorrows, decide to follow the impossible-seeming dreams that God will start to show you. Your pain will recede as your heart gets to dream again.

CALLED TO DO WHAT YOU CANNOT PERFORM

It's true that your God-given dreams will be impossible to perform—without him. You will need to listen for his subtle direction in order to keep pace with the Holy Spirit.

He can equip anybody to keep in step with him: young or old, seasoned or brand-new Christian, educated or uneducated, male or female. Look what our God did for Joseph's great-grandfather, Abraham, who was a childless, elderly nomad when God visited him. Nobody would have called him a patriarch then! God pronounced impossible goals to Abraham, promising him countless descendants (among them, Joseph) who would make a huge difference in the future of human civilization. And old Abraham, suspending his understandable skepticism, went along with the plan. He could not have known how it would play out. He just took one step at a time, which is the same way any of us walk.

To his eternal credit, Abraham took hold of the very words that God had given him without even having the benefit (as we do) of knowing these words of Jesus: "Man shall not live by bread alone, but by every word that proceeds from the mouth of God" (Matthew 4:4 NKJV). The word *proceeds* in the Greek is stated in an ongoing, active tense: "Man lives by every word that has proceeded, does proceed, and will proceed from the mouth of God." In other words, if you intend to follow God's directives, you must stay as close as possible to him. You will be able to listen well enough only if you're close enough.

You must cultivate a *relationship* with your Father God if you want to undertake his plan for your future. What does any good father want with his children? Good communication. There you have it. The key to moving out of your wilderness time and into something new is your relationship with God himself. He's holding the plan for your life, and he wants to help you keep up with him. I'm just trying to keep up with the ever-moving Holy Spirit!

LET GOD FULFILL WHAT HE HAS PROMISED

Dare to trust God both to give you a dream and to fulfill it. The Bible is clear that "the one who calls you is faithful, and he will do it" (1 Thessalonians 5:24 NIV). God has not abandoned you to your difficult circumstances. Decide to drop your crutches and follow your Lord. God's plans for you may well seem impossible, but you will be going forward on *his* strength and wisdom, not your own.

If you get confused or discouraged, review how God has worked in other people, especially your forerunners in the faith in the Bible. Read between the lines of their stories. Feel the heartbeat of the people who went through daunting—even terrifying—events, tenaciously hanging onto seemingly impossible promises from God. Yes, they made mistakes too (just as we do). Yet God kept taking care of them. They lost hope at times. They took matters into their own hands. They failed. But God would not relent.

A promise is a promise. When he makes up his mind, he stays the course. He engineers circumstances. He sends encouragement. He revives dreams. He infuses hearts with hope. He also provides patience. Your dream might take a lifetime; Abraham's certainly did. Character-building is an inevitable part of the process, and we should welcome it despite the fact that it may not always feel good.

Let God fulfill his particular promises for you, which will differ from his promises for somebody else. We will all be able to learn the same principles from our journeys with God, but our circumstances will not be the same. Some people around you will seem to have it so *easy*. Why must your assignment include such intense pain? Don't dwell on the disparity. Instead, help yourself to a good dose of truth from the Word, Psalm 37, for example:

> Do not fret because of those who are evil or be
> envious of those who do wrong;
> for like the grass they will soon wither, like green
> plants they will soon die away.
> *Trust* in the Lord and do good; *dwell* in the land
> and enjoy safe pasture.
> Take delight in the Lord, and he will give you the
> desires of your heart.
> *Commit* your way to the Lord; trust in him and he
> will do this...
> Be still before the Lord and wait patiently... (Psalm
> 37:1–7 NIV, emphasis added)

Steer clear of fretfulness and envy. When you discover that you are starting to get anxious and easily aggravated (or worse), remember that you belong to God. Ask him to help you understand your reactions. Place yourself in his strong hands and repent of trying to take care of your world without him. You can recover your footing with three key words from Psalm 37: Trust. Dwell. Commit.

Trust in your Lord anew. Don't put the cart before the horse, trying so hard to believe in your expectations regarding God's promise that you pull back from believing in the faithfulness of the promiser himself. He will fulfill his promises—in his own time and way.

Dwell in God and in his provision for you. Stir up your heart to thank him for everything. He himself is your secure dwelling place, and he will always be there for you.

Commit yourself to him all over again. Confess your fears and put them aside in favor of trusting that he will see you through. The God who put the dream in your heart promises to fortify you every step of the way. Do you believe that? Okay, then that's something you can stand on!

HEROINE OF HOPE: JACKIE PULLINGER

In 1966, a young British woman named Jackie Pullinger brought the hope of Christ to one of the darkest places on earth, the walled city of Kowloon in Hong Kong. On her own, without the support of a missionary society, she prayed and labored for decades, having had a dream of working for God in Hong Kong. Governing authorities had forsaken and ignored the walled city of Kowloon, and it had become entirely lawless. Its hovels housed thirty to sixty thousand residents (no one could take a census, so no one knew for sure), and its maze of fetid alleyways were crowded with opium dens, heroin huts, brothels, illegal gambling houses, porn theaters, and more. Days were dark in every way—the sun rarely penetrated the cracks between the rickety structures—and nights were worse, with endless vice and violence. Public services were nonexistent. Residents had to illegally tap into electricity from sources outside alls, and sanitary facilities were unknown.

Jackie's failures seemed to outstrip her successes, especially at first. But by the power of the Holy Spirit, her one-woman crusade led to the conversion of untold numbers of people who had been hopeless and helpless all their lives. God had given her a dream—a vision to make an eternal positive difference in the lives of the disenfranchised—and eventually, she founded a vibrant church and a highly successful drug rehabilitation program called St. Stephen's Society, which has continued to expand to this day.

Kowloon was razed in 1993, and its former site is now a park, but as Jesus said, "The poor will always be with you." There will always be wretchedness and addiction. Jackie's work of bringing hope to the hopeless in Hong Kong and beyond goes on. Her hardships and adventures could fill a book, and they have.[4] Jackie is another amazing modern-day heroine of hope.

At an early age, Jackie let the Holy Spirit deposit a world-changing desire in her heart. Is your heart postured to receive the dream God has for you? Are you acting the dream God has already placed your heart?

PRAYER

Father, I am grateful for my past, but I
need fresh pages to turn. I open my heart to
you so that you can rekindle old dreams and
put new ones into my heart. I want to be able
to follow you into the future you have planned
for me, and I need your help so that I can hear
your directives and persist through hard times. I
have a dream of being a source of life for those

---

4   Notably, two titles: *Chasing the Dragon* and *Crack in the Wall.*

around me, and I believe that you are develop-
ing that dream more every day. I find my hope
in you alone. Amen.

DISCOVERING HOPE TAKEAWAYS

Chapter 8
Let God Put a Dream in Your Heart

✦ To move into the future with hope, you need new dreams and goals. Read Psalm 37:1–7.

✦ Don't waste your sorrows; let them drive you to follow the dreams that God will show you.

✦ Confess your faith in God's faithfulness and be quick to obey; your pain will recede as you start to follow God's direction.

✦ Patiently welcome the character-building that comes with the journey.

CHAPTER 9

NEVER, NEVER, NEVER GIVE UP!

Return to the stronghold, O prisoners who have the hope;
this very day I am declaring that I will restore double to you.
ZECHARIAH 9:12 NASB

It was September 2008, and I was about to go to North Carolina to minister at Mahesh and Bonnie Chavda's church. My wife had been battling cancer for four intense years, and she was very weak. By that time, we had a full-time healthcare giver who stayed in our home and took care of her around the clock. Before I went to the airport, I went into the bedroom to sit on the edge of her hospital bed to say goodbye. She was conscious, but her condition was very poor.

"Hey Annie, I've got to go to North Carolina to be with Mahesh and Bonnie." They were our lifelong friends, and in fact, it was Mahesh who had prayed prophetically that we would be able to have children when we couldn't.

With difficulty, Michal Ann responded, "Oh, good! Tell them hello for me." Then she wanted to do what she usually did, which was to bless me for my travels, but she was so feeble she needed my help to lift her hand up to put it on my head. Off I went with her blessing.

I was going to be gone for a few days, and while I was there, I wanted to also pay a visit to Bob Jones, who was like a father figure to me. (He has since graduated to be with the Lord.) He and his wife lived close by, so I went to their house on my second day. As soon as I walked in the door, Bob said abruptly, "Well, you're graduating." I did not necessarily like hearing what I thought I was hearing, but I accepted it. He clarified: "You're going to graduate into the realm of compassion." I remembered the name of Michal Ann's ministry, Compassion Acts. We chatted about that and other things for a little while. Right before the end of my short visit, Bob made another prophetic statement: "By the way, your wife has one last word to give you."

This was a Saturday afternoon. I went back to the evening meeting at the Chavda's church for the Saturday evening service. At that closing session of the conference on Saturday evening, it was Mahesh's turn to minister, and I found my seat on the front row. At the beginning of worship, someone walked up to me very fast and handed me a card in a turquoise-blue envelope. It seemed like he said, "This is a word to you from your wife." I quickly opened it up. Inside was a card, and the front of it read, "'Never, never, never give up'—Winston Churchill."

It did sound like something Michal Ann would say. I put the card back into the envelope without reading the inside and turned around to thank the person who had delivered it. I wanted to say, "Who are you? How did you get this? I want to talk to you." I looked all around, but the messenger was gone. Nobody around me seemed to have seen him, before or afterward. I tucked the card away in my Bible so I could concentrate on the worship and Mahesh's message.

After I ministered at the Sunday morning service the next day, I flew home. As soon as I walked in the door, I learned that my wife had fallen into a coma while I was away and that it appeared she would not last long. So the time had come. I excused the health-care worker so I could spend one last night in our bedroom with my Annie alone, just watching and waiting and telling her how dear she was. I knew that her spirit would be able to hear me even if her body was comatose.

At some point in the wee hours of the morning, I laid my head on her chest and told her about Bob's prophetic statement about her giving me a last word. Of course, she could not respond, so I had to believe that her last word would have to come by means of a dream or in some other way. I sang over her and prayed over her and gave her to the Lord. A few hours later, on the morning of September 15, 2008, she breathed her last.

My family's life became a whirlwind as we arranged two funerals, one in Nashville and one back in Missouri where we laid her body to rest beside her parents in the peaceful rural setting of Dover. I completely forgot about the card in the blue envelope.

Six weeks later, I was already traveling again. I had cancelled one scheduled international trip, but I felt I could manage this one to Seoul, South Korea. As it turned out, the Day of Atonement happened to fall in the middle of the conference. That day is the most holy day in the Jewish calendar and has always been special to me because often over the years, the Lord has spoken to me on that day. This one was no exception. That night in the hotel, I had a sig-

124 • TELL YOUR HEART TO SING AGAIN

nificant dream. In the dream, I relived that Saturday night meeting at Mahesh and Bonnie Chavda's church in slow motion. I woke up right at five in the morning while in the dream I was looking around for the person who had handed me the card. Then the clear voice of the Holy Spirit spoke to me, *I sent my angel to you to give you your wife's last word.*

I thought, *That was an angel? No wonder I couldn't find the person afterward!* Then suddenly I remembered that I still had the card right inside the Bible I carry with me everywhere I go. So I jumped out of bed, full of energy (definitely unusual for me), found my Bible, and opened it up to find the blue envelope. There it was! This time, I didn't just read the Churchill quote on the front; I hurried to open the card to see what it said on the inside. The inside was even better, because it was so personal. It read: "I'll never, never, never stop cheering for you."

I understood that the Churchill quote could apply to any-body—to each of you who are reading this right now. But the inside message was even more meaningful now that my wife had become part of the "great cloud of witnesses" (Hebrews 12:1). Her last word to me and to our children was that she was going to be cheering for us from the balcony of heaven through every difficulty that would come our way.

I turned the card over to see what it might say on the back. It was just an ordinary Hallmark card, but I noticed that it had been manufactured in Kansas City, Missouri. Even that held significance for me because that was where Michal Ann and I had lived a good part of our married life. I carefully put the card back in my Bible, which is where it has stayed ever since, so that I can reread its hope-building message as often as I want to.

KEEP YOUR HAND TO THE PLOW

Sometimes the words on that card kind of haunt me. Sometimes they guide me. But they always bring me hope, and I think they can bring hope to you as well. Never, never, never give up. Never give up on finding hope. Never give up on your dreams. Never give up on God. Never give up on the church. Never give up on your family. Never give up on yourself.

Even when your dreams do not come true and God seems far away, don't ever give up. Believe that he cares for you and that he intends to bring good out of everything. If you keep your hand in his, he will definitely help you "keep your hand to the plow." Do not be one of those people who looks back with longing and regret. Remember what Jesus said: "No one who puts a hand to the plow and looks back is fit for service in the kingdom of God" (Luke 9:62 NIV). That is a strong statement. Sometimes it will take everything you have to carry on, but God will help you.

Think of it this way: As you keep on keeping on, know that you will always find the hope you need in *front* of you, not behind you. That reminds me of my friend Danny Gokey (see chapter 7) and the title of his book and song *Hope in Front of Me.* Always keep in mind that hope is up there somewhere in front of you, so the important thing is to commit yourself to keep looking straight ahead. With your hand on the plow, do not turn to look back over your shoulder, thinking that you might have missed something. God's heart-healing hope is what you need, not scraps from your past. You can never anticipate what kind of package your hope will come in, but I can tell you that it will not be too small. I am still investigating and unwrapping mine, still on my journey of becoming a new man.

The best will not have passed you by because the best will *never* be behind you. Yes, you may have lost some very good things, such as health or loved ones or comfortable circumstances. But you are not supposed to spend your energy to steward the "best of the past," nor are you supposed to try to read between the lines in order to explain everything completely. Your life journey may never make sense in natural, logical terms, but you can expect it to bring you all the way to heaven with your hope-strengthened spirit intact and your heart engaged with love for the Lord Jesus Christ.

Never compare your journey with someone else's since everyone's journey will be distinctly personal. Just keep your focus forward as clearly and steadfastly as you can. Without knowing yet where God is leading you, declare the truth to yourself, *I have a redemptive purpose and calling in this life! God is not finished with me yet!*

THE PROMISE: I WILL RESTORE

God can and will do what only God can do: he will restore. Will he restore the exact things you have lost? No. But better than that, he will restore *double* to you. This may sound like too much to swallow, but I am taking it straight from the Bible: "Return to the stronghold, you prisoners of hope. Even today I declare that I will restore double to you" (Zechariah 9:12 NKJV). Every time you return to the secure stronghold of hope, reaffirm God's declaration over you. It is a promise. He says, "I will restore double to *you*," "I *will* restore double to you," "I will *restore* double to you," "I will restore *double* to you." I graft this word into my soul every day!

We need restoration, don't we? We might find ourselves in a temporary state of hopelessness. In spite of our difficult circumstances. God's word says we are to return and become prisoners to hope. The fact is that every individual is going to be a prisoner to something or someone at all times, whether hope or despair, light or darkness. Before we first gave our lives to Jesus, we used to be prisoners of sin. We gladly traded that kind of bondage for another—we became bondservants of our Savior. As our reliance upon him grows, the more we become his joyful "prisoners." We are captives to our revelation. Today, I am a prisoner of hope, and that is one prison sentence I am not planning on escaping!

We spend our entire Christian lives "working out our salvation" (Philippians 2:12), learning to put aside our old ways of slavery as we become freely dependent upon Jesus. It is a long learning process. When extreme difficulties arise, we tend to revert to our old "masters," but such tests of our loyalty can help to reinforce our commitment to Jesus Christ.

Ultimately, we want to be prisoners of *hope,* and in order to come back to that stronghold of hope, we need to remember that God is always hopeful toward us. He is the Messiah of the Jewish people and of all people, and he says, "All the day long I have stretched out My hands to a disobedient and obstinate people" (Romans 10:21 NASB, quoting Isaiah 65:2). He does not say, "I have folded my arms. I gave them a chance and they rejected me, so I refuse to ever reach out to them again." He wants to restore you to hope and a double portion of his grace.

He encourages us to walk in the light that we have, not giving up on it even when it seems insufficient. Our present level of revelation will lead to more if we stick with it and do not disdain it. Remember what it is like for the caterpillar that is in the middle of his transition of metamorphosis (chapter 4). That is not the time to

quit, is it? Your experience may not yet match your hopeful expectation, but hang on to God and it will.

There will always be things that you will not excel at, and you may think that faith and hope are just not your thing. But practice yields increase and improvement. Practice taking one step of faith at a time. Practice believing that what the Lord has said is true, even for your messed-up life. Return to him with all of your heart, soul, mind, and strength because He alone is the source of your life and your hope.

JAIL BREAK TIME

It is as if God has handed you a Get Out of Jail Free card, like the one in the board game of *Monopoly*. If you remember that you have it, you can use that card when you need to, or you can just hang onto it and stay in jail. I wonder sometimes why we end up doing that. We stay imprisoned and immobilized in our fears or depression, unable even to pray, when the whole time we have in our pocket God's Get Out of Jail Free card, which has a cross on it. We forget, until someone reminds us, that God has sent us viable hope of freedom and that it has no expiration date. We do not have to pay for our freedom. The Lord has done that for us, and he sets us free as many times as necessary. He is the one "Who executes justice for the oppressed; who gives food to the hungry. The Lord sets the prisoners free" (Psalm 146:7 NASB).

In his hometown synagogue in Nazareth, Jesus proclaimed the words of Isaiah, and he intended for his hearers (which includes us) to take them personally:

> The Spirit of the Lord is upon Me,
> Because He has anointed Me

To preach the gospel to the poor;
He has sent Me to heal the brokenhearted,
To proclaim liberty to the captives
And recovery of sight to the blind,
To set at liberty those who are oppressed;
To proclaim the acceptable year of the Lord. (Luke 4:18–19 NKJV, quoting Isaiah 61:1)

When you realize that it is time to break out of an emotional and spiritual prison, you need to turn your attention to the present and to the future, which is where you will find hope. It is perfectly okay to acknowledge what happened in the past, both the laurels and the failures. But resist the temptation to try to resurrect any of it, even the good parts. You have to step out of the shadows of the past, including shadows of greatness. You may have won an Academy Award or a Nobel Peace Prize, but what does it matter for today?

 What matters is how you finish the race. And you run the race 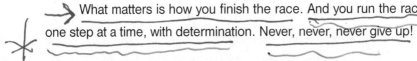 one step at a time, with determination. Never, never, never give up!

HERO OF HOPE: WINSTON CHURCHILL

I chose Sir Winston Churchill for this chapter simply because of his words on my card in its blue envelope. Winston Churchill may have had some personal character flaws, but lack of determination was not one of them. In a time of crisis, he was perfectly suited to bringing hope to others, even in the bleakest of circumstances. Churchill served in a number of leadership roles for fifty years, and Americans best know him as the prime minister of England during World War II.

Churchill refused to back down from threats, and he never

turned tail to run from danger. According to biographer Stephen Mansfield, Churchill exemplified a number of what he termed "pillars of greatness." He was a thinker, a dreamer, a man of action, a giver, and more. Mansfield wrote:

> The chief lesson of Churchill's leadership is that greatness is a product of character, of matters like loyalty, sacrifice, endurance, and courage … Perhaps if men like Churchill are indeed remembered and heard in generations to come, it will mean nothing less than the inspiration to rise above the commonplace in the service of mankind. When this inspiration fills the hearts of leaders yet unborn and they will seek to master the lessons of greatness, they will undoubtedly grow to revere the name and the life of Sir Winston Churchill.[5]

Another word for "inspiration to rise above the commonplace" is *hope.* Churchill believed that his strongest weapon was his pen, and the line I have on my card, "Never, never, never give up," is one of his most often-quoted ones. It comes from a speech he gave in 1941 titled "The Unrelenting Struggle." He was talking about the current war effort at the time, but his message could just as easily apply to any of us in our unrelenting struggle against hopelessness. When we are buffeted by confusing, challenging, and sometimes violent circumstances, hopelessness becomes enemy number one.

Anyone who can rise above the smoke of the battlefield long enough to get a lungful of the hope-infused atmosphere of heaven

5   Stephen Mansfield, *Never Give In: The Extraordinary Character of Winston Churchill* (Nashville, Tenn.: Cumberland House, 1997), 224–225.

will win every time. And hopefully that person will become another hero or heroine of hope, inspiring others as well.

PRAYER

Father, by the grace that you alone can supply, I choose to keep my hands on the plow and not look back over my shoulder. I declare that hope is in front of me and that you will use all I have gone through for the sake of my redemption and for the benefit of others. I need you to strengthen me with your faith, hope, courage, and love. Help me to keep looking forward into your eternal promises and give me supernatural fortitude. I put my hope in you for every step I must take. Thank you, gracious Father, and amen.

DISCOVERING HOPE TAKEAWAYS

Chapter 9
Never, Never, Never Give Up!

✦ Never give up on finding hope. Never give up on God, who can bring good out of anything. Never give up, even when you get disappointed.

✦ Without knowing yet where God is leading you, declare the truth to yourself: *God is not finished with me yet! I have a redemptive purpose and calling in this life!*

✦ God has promised to restore to you more than you have lost. Read Zechariah 9:12.

✦ Practice taking one step of faith at a time. Practice believing that what the Lord has said is true.

✦ Turn your attention to the future, which is where you will find hope.

CHAPTER 10

No Matter What Comes, God Is Good

I pray that the eyes of your heart may be enlightened, so that you will
know what is the hope of His calling, what are the riches of the glory
of His inheritance in the saints, and what is the surpassing greatness of
His power toward us who believe.
EPHESIANS 1:18–19 NASB

I had what you might call a "divine appointment" while I was working on this chapter. One morning, the Holy Spirit interrupted my
thinking with the strong sense that I should leave the house and
drive over to a local commercial establishment called The Factory,
where I would meet somebody.

I was reluctant to stir myself; I was feeling kind of down, and
it seemed as if it might be a waste of time. But the Holy Spirit was
persistent, so I went out the door just the same because I have
learned that these things often prove to be from God.

The Factory is a handful of upscale shops, places to eat,

and other enterprises housed in a collection of refurbished warehouses. I decided to head to a café I knew, where I could order something and just sit a while. So I got my organic, freshly made juice and a little bowl filled with nuts and fruits, and I sat down with it. Another customer came in, and he stopped and looked at me. "Are you, like, could you maybe be James Goll?"

I did my Clark Kent routine because you never know who you might be talking to: "Well, sometimes." He asked if we could sit down together.

Turns out, he was an old friend. We hardly recognized each other because it had been at least twenty-five years since we had last seen each other. Even though both of us had lived in the same general area for the past eighteen years, our paths had not crossed. We had actually gone together on a mission trip to Moscow all those years ago. Since we had last seen each other, both of us had gone gray (in my case, also sparse on top), and it wasn't only because of the passage of years.

We caught each other up on all that had happened in the past two decades. I told him my story in brief, and then he told me his. This man was absolutely broken. He had been married when we had traveled to Russia, but afterward he had gone through a divorce, lost his job, and a lot more. His ex-wife had just died two years ago, and now he was grappling with some new challenges. He was still a believer, but he had pretty much lost his hope. Everything seemed to keep going so very wrong.

I thought of Job, so I shared with him that passage from the Book of Job that I reviewed in chapter 4 of this book: "For there is hope for a tree, if it is cut down, that it will sprout again, and that its tender shoots will not cease" (Job 14:7 NKJV). I also told him to read the next two verses, although I was actually uncertain about what they said. As it turns out, those two verses are quite significant: "Though its root may grow old in the earth, and its stump may die in the ground, yet at the scent of water it will bud and bring forth branches like a plant" (Job 14:8–9 NKJV).

We were sort of like two old stumps, he and I, somewhat lifeless and seemingly uncared-for. And yet the message of our always-good God is that he wants to bring life back. He can revive and restore even what appears to be cut down to its roots. At the mere scent of divine water, God's miracles can happen!

Neither of us had experienced full restoration yet, but we could have hope. By bringing us together in a "chance" meeting, God brought both of us closer to being able once again to "bud and bring forth branches like a plant." Out of his goodness, God showed us that he cares, even if we still look like a couple of weathered stumps in the ground (at a health food café, no less!).

GOD IS GOOD

That brings me to the theme of this chapter: No matter what comes, God is good. He doesn't stop being good when my life falls apart, even when I happen to be at fault for some of my troubles. He doesn't stop being good when I forget he is good or if I never understand in the first place that he is good. God is good, period.

Each one of us needs to ask the Holy Spirit to graft that truth into our souls because otherwise we will continue to wobble in our faith. We do not yet know God anywhere near as well as he knows us, but he would like us to come closer to knowing him well. To know him is to love him and to believe that he cares.

To help myself remember this truth, I long ago adopted as one of my life verses the passage I placed at the beginning of this chapter. I pray it for myself on a daily basis because I know that unless God enlightens the eyes of my heart, I will never arrive at the hope of his calling, nor will I have any comprehension of the riches of his goodness toward me and toward anyone who believes in him.

SEEING WITH THE EYES OF YOUR HEART

This verse has been a very real guiding light for me on my journey through some dark territory. Many times, I can only glimpse its light at the end of the tunnel I'm walking (or crawling) in, but it is God's light, and I know it. The more I pray those verses, the more certain my steps become and the brighter the light grows.

Sometimes I have felt I was walking in a trackless wasteland, as if I have not only lost my roadmap but also run off the road—quite a long way back. It's as if my difficulties have almost started defining me, giving me an unwanted new (and crummy-looking) map to work from. I know, I know ... the difficulties don't really alter my God-given roadmap. But they were so unexpected. Now I'm seeing all sorts of hidden side alleys, unforeseen obstacles, and invisible construction zones that never showed up on that old map. This gives me all the more reason to learn to see with the eyes of my heart. When I view my life from God's perspective and let him shine his glorious light on it, all of the detours and potholes start to make sense.

The verses at the beginning of this chapter have kept me moving toward God's guiding light. Even in the midst of the worst storms, they have helped me catch sight of the light in the distance so that I can turn in the right direction. For over ten years, I prayed those verses several times a day for myself, and I still pray them at least weekly. I use those words to invite God to open the eyes of my heart.

The "eyes of my heart" give me special sight so that I can see behind the sometimes-dire things that my natural eyes show me. I want the eyes of my heart to keep functioning well even if the rest of me should get sick because the eyes of my heart help me see the riches of the glory of God, and they help me recall how good He is. With the eyes of my heart "enlightened," I can see with hope. When they are darkened or blindfolded—which can happen just as easily as it can with my natural eyes—I lose my way. You know how many things can go wrong with your natural eyes that may not render them completely blind but that impede clear vision: near-sightedness, farsightedness, cataracts, glaucoma. (I could preach a sermon about eyes, and maybe I should!)

I want the eyes of my heart—my spirit-eyes—to be clearly focused and "single," as the King James Bible puts it (Luke 11:34). To paraphrase Paul's prayer for the Ephesians, "I pray that the eyes of my heart will be opened so that great light can come in and so that a picture, a vision for the future, can develop within the hope, the positive expectation of good. Amen."

The Lord highlighted this for me in a personal way. One time after my wife had died, I got up early in the morning, and I was praying those verses on my bed in the bedroom, across from some glass French doors screened with venetian blinds. At the very moment when I was praying that my eyes would be enlightened, the rising sun pierced between the slats of the blinds and bathed my face in sunlight. I was delighted! It was a perfect picture of how this works. I still didn't know how to make my next decisions, but I knew where the light was. My confusion lifted, and I just knew everything was going to be all right because God is always good, and he cares for me. He is in charge of my life, and He knows what he's doing.

Take my advice—whenever you go through difficult times, pray the Bible. It works. It opens the eyes of your heart. Don't ask me how it works, but somehow two plus two equals five. With God, all things are possible (Matthew 19:26; Mark 10:27), and he easily factors in our human weaknesses. He is both sovereign and providential—and he providentially chose to give us human beings a free will, risking our likely revolt. He knows what we do to each other. He knows what the devil does to us. He's still God, and he loves us. He knows how everything will come out in the end. He takes the hands of those who ask him to guide them, and the shepherd of our soul will restore to them the years that seemed to have been lost forever.

ASK BIG

When you pray to God to know more about the "riches of the glory of His inheritance," you aren't just asking for an open parking space downtown. You are asking for something so big you may not be able to grasp it. Don't let the majesty and mystery of it cause you to draw back with hesitation. Just pray. That's what Moses did:

> Moses said, "Now show me your glory."
> And the Lord said, "I will cause all my goodness to pass in front of you, and I will proclaim my name, the Lord, in your presence. I will have mercy on whom I will have mercy, and I will have compassion on whom I will have compassion." (Exodus 33:18–19 NIV)

God had just told Moses that he knew him by name and that he had found favor, which so increased Moses's confidence in his relationship with God that he dared to ask the impossible. God reminded him that no one could see his face and live (Exodus 33:20), but Moses upheld his request anyway. He did not feel that anyone needed to ask on his behalf, and he did not ask for a vicarious experience of God's glory ("Show my brother Aaron your glory and let me just watch—in case he gets fried"). Moses asked for something that he might not survive, not because he was into extreme sports but simply because he was so buoyed up by God's affirmation. His hope was translated into full faith.

I see great significance in God's response to Moses: "I will cause all my goodness to pass in front of you." In front, where his eyes could see, God's glorious *goodness* would pass. And it did. Where? Right in front of him!

I believe that we can pray for big things like that too. We can pray for displays of the goodness of God to pass in front of the eyes of our hearts. We can pray for demonstrations of the goodness of God to flood our soul and minds. We can get excited to think of what he might do in response to our prayers. Remember, hope is a confident anticipation of good. To find hope is to discover a major aspect of God's nature: his goodness.

LOOKING FOR GOODNESS

The story of God's goodness passing in front of Moses is in the Old Testament. To bring it over into the New Testament, we need to look no further than Peter's description of Jesus of Nazareth:

> You know of Jesus of Nazareth, how God anointed Him with the Holy Spirit and with power, and how He went about doing good and healing all who were oppressed by the devil, for God was with Him. (Acts 10:38 NASB)

To this day, Jesus is going about doing good, although we may question that fact when something bad happens. Sometimes

I have wondered if he is off on vacation or sitting regally on his throne instead of helping me here on this messed-up earth. But when I go back to the written Word of God, my misconceptions clear up. Jesus is always going about doing good because he said that he would never leave us or forsake us (Hebrews 13:5). He sent his Holy Spirit not to touch our lives only from time to time, but to dwell within us (1 Corinthians 3:16; Romans 8:11). Right where we are, Jesus is always doing good and doing it well.

GOD C.A.R.E.S.

A pastor friend, Alex Seeley of The Belonging Co., a local church that I attend in the Nashville area, gave me permission to use her memorable acronym: C.A.R.E.S. Each letter stands for an aspect of our seeking God's goodness for our lives:

> C—Cry out.
> A—Appeal to his nature.
> R—Remember what he has done in the past.
> E—Enlarge God over your circumstances.
> S—Sing.

C—Cry out. You don't have to deny the pain; it helps to cry out to God in the midst of it. You have to cry some tears in order to give God something to put into his special bottle: "You keep track of all my sorrows. You have collected all my tears in your bottle. You have recorded each one in your book" (Psalm 56:8 NLT). I like to say it this way: Don't live a bottled-up life; give God something to bottle up. This is the first step on the path of recovery, and you will not be able to find hope if you omit it. It is okay to cry out in absolute desperation. In fact, it is preferable to cry out in desperation. When you are at the end of your rope, you know you need God and that you cannot do enough on your own strength to make a difference. That's a perfect starting place, and it's the best way to find out for yourself that God cares about *you*, personally.

A—Appeal to his nature. Tell yourself, tell the enemy, and remind God of his divine nature—the attributes of his character—his goodness, his faithfulness, his loving-kindness. Find particular verses in Scripture that help you recount his qualities. "Who is like You among the gods, O Lord? Who is like You, majestic in holiness, awesome in praises, working wonders!" (Exodus 15:11 NASB).

R—Remember what he has done in the past. If you can't remember a single thing that he has done for you in the past or if you run out of ideas, simply resort to the Bible. Recite some of God's mighty deeds from both the Old and New Testaments and let that prime the pump of your own memories. Recount how God sent the flood but preserved good Noah, his family, and enough animals to repopulate the earth. Recount how Jesus Christ went about doing good—healing the blind eyes and raising the dead. Recall how he died on the cross while we were yet sinners. Then remember the time you didn't know how you were going to pay your rent, but somehow God sent the money. Remember the time he made the sun shine in your eyes through the venetian blinds to show you that he cares. Remember what he has done for you personally.

E—Enlarge God over your circumstances. All of this will help you see how big God is. Magnify him—in all senses of the word! Glorify him and praise him and make his bigness known to yourself and others. "Magnify the Lord with me! Let's praise his name together!" (Psalm 34:3 NET). You need to get the right perspective. Your tragedy or loss is not bigger than God. He's always bigger and better than any personal (or even global) problem you can come up with.

S—Sing! With all of that build-up, you may already be singing. But in case you aren't, let me urge you to open your mouth and let out a shout of praise—even before your circumstances change for the better. Look at this exhortation:

> "Sing, O barren,
> You who have not borne!
> Break forth into singing, and cry aloud,
> You who have not labored with child!
> For more are the children of the desolate
> Than the children of the married woman," says the
> Lord. (Isaiah 54:1 NKJV, quoted in Galatians 4:27)

Your singing will change the spiritual climate around you so that authentic faith can arise. You may not feel happy. But you will be resolute. It will be a true sacrifice of praise. Something about this response changes things and shakes them up. That's what it did literally for Paul and Silas when they were in prison in Philippi (Acts 16). They were singing God's praises in the middle of the night, and an earthquake came. They got set free, and their worshipful steadfastness converted the jailer and his entire household.

You might decide to go through this C.A.R.E.S routine daily for a while. If you do, you will find that it is good medicine for your soul. Hope will rise with the morning sun and joy won't be far behind.

HERO OF HOPE: NICK VUJICIC

You may have heard of Nick Vujicic (VOY-*i-chich*), an amazing Australian Christian who was born without arms or legs. His Christian parents were dismayed at their newborn son's condition. Nick writes: "At first they assumed that there was no hope and no future for someone like me, that I would never live a normal or productive life."[6] But he struggled through his growing up years, and God began to show him the great good that could come out of his situation.

He lives in the United States now; he's married to a beautiful woman, and they are proud parents of their own biological children. Nick wrote a book called *Life Without Limits: Inspiration for a Ridiculously Good Life,* and he likes to say, "No arms, no legs, no limits!"

Today Nick has a growing resume and an impressive speaking itinerary all over the world. One of his primary messages is how to "love the perfectly imperfect you," which anybody can profit from learning how to do, even those of us who have both arms and legs. On his list of what you need to have in order to "live without limits," Nick included "a hope so strong it cannot be diminished."[7] He went on to give hope an entire chapter, and he quoted Martin Luther King, Jr.: "Everything that is done in the world is done by hope." Where does Nick get that kind of hope? The same place you and I do—from God, the one who holds the future in his capable, almighty hands. A hero of hope like Nick knows that his own considerable limitations suit him perfectly to experience God's amazing goodness and the surpassing greatness of his power toward us who believe. Lord, I am amazed by you.

6   Nick Vujicic, *Life Without Limits: Inspiration for a Ridiculously Good Life* (Colorado Springs: Waterbrook, 2010), vii.

7   Vujicic, ix.

PRAYER

Father, I declare that no matter what comes, your character and nature remain constant, and you are good all the time. Indeed, your mercies endure forever. I cast my cares upon you because I believe that you care for me. I enter into your presence with thanksgiving and praise, and I cry out to you like Moses of old, "Show me your glory! Let your goodness pass in front of us." In Jesus Christ's great name. Amen.

DISCOVERING HOPE TAKEAWAYS

Chapter 10
No Matter What Comes, God Is Good

✦ Hope is a confident anticipation of good, and finding hope means discovering that no matter what, God is good. He doesn't stop being good when your life falls apart or when you forget he is good. God is good—period.

✦ When you view your life from God's perspective, the detours and potholes start to make sense.

✦ Ask him to enlighten the "eyes of your heart." Read Ephesians 1:18–19.

✦ Pray the Bible. Pray big. Pray C.A.R.E.S:

- C—Cry out.

- A—Appeal to his nature.

- R—Remember what he has done in the past.

- E—Enlarge God over your circumstances.

- S—Sing.

CHAPTER 11

BEAUTY FROM ASHES

To appoint unto them that mourn in Zion, to give unto them beauty
for ashes, the oil of joy for mourning, the garment of praise for the spirit
of heaviness; that they might be called the trees of righteousness,
the planting of the Lord, that he might be glorified.
ISAIAH 61:3 KJV

God is the master artist, and he paints beautiful pictures. Some of
the most beautiful and profound views we can see in this world are
shaped by clouds—storm clouds in particular. The storm, however,
is not the final picture God paints in the sky. At the end of the storm,
there is a golden sky fitted with a rainbow of promise filling the air.
He really does bring beauty out of ashes. Only God can do that!

Our mess is an opportunity for his next miracle. Remember the ugly duckling? As it matures, it becomes a beautiful swan.
Remember the caterpillar crawling lowly on the ground? That is
not the final state of this God-ordained creature. It becomes hungry, spins a chrysalis and develops a hiding place, goes through
a meltdown, and finally emerges a beautiful butterfly capable of

spreading its wings and catching the wind to soar. The Holy Spirit really does make all things new!

WHAT ARE ASHES ANYWAY?

He gives us beauty for ashes. But what are ashes anyway? I believe there are four things about ashes that are important for us to remember:

First, ashes are evidence of a previous fire. You might be feeling temporarily like nothing more right now than a pile of ashes, but that means previously there was a fire burning brightly. It all depends upon your perspective. You can look at the pile of your life and only see it as completely burned up. You can take that perspective and go into not just mourning but also sorrow, entering the downward spiral that will take you all the way into the pity party. And remember, that's not pretty at any age.

Second, ashes are evidence of a sacrifice. Now this is how we can see the ashes if we look at them with a redemptive interpretation. Through that interpretation, we know that our sacrifice releases power. This is a principle throughout the Word of God. That's why the Lord will say things to us like, *Add fasting to your prayer*. That's a sacrifice. How differently would you look at the ashes in your life if you saw that they are releasing power into your life?

Third, do you know that ashes can help make an infertile field fertile? Two of the events we can witness in the earth that cause the greatest devastation—forest fires and volcanic eruptions—both lead to some of the most fertile soil you can get. In these cases, ashes become a potent ingredient that helps make the desert blossom.

Fourth, ashes carry an aroma that ascends. Remember that Noah took eight people, counting himself, onto the great ship.

He took the animals, the clean and the unclean, the twos and the multiples, and then the flood comes. They were probably tossed around. They lost almost everything they had ever known. And, eventually, the rain stopped, the ark settled, and Noah sent out a dove. It came back the first time, the second time it brought back an olive leaf, and the third time it did not come back. This was the sign that the waters had receded, and Noah could leave the ark.

The first thing Noah did after he and his family came back to the renewed earth was offer a sacrifice to the Lord. Scripture says regarding that sacrifice, "And the Lord was pleased with the aroma of the sacrifice" (Genesis 8:21 NLT). Why did he smell the aroma? Because ashes carry an aroma; they ascend. They don't just stay here, but they carry the aroma of our sacrifice to God.

The last thing God breathed in became an element of the next thing God exhaled. God breathed in the pleasing aroma of sacrifice, and he exhaled the declaration, "'I will never again curse the ground on account of man ... and I will never again destroy every living thing'" (Genesis 8:21 NASB). He then continues by renewing his covenant with mankind and makes even further promise that "never again shall the water become a flood to destroy all flesh" (Genesis 9:15 NASB).

God even sets a rainbow in the sky to remind everyone, including himself, of his promise. Every time you see that colorful bow in the sky, God is telling you that at the end of the storm, there is a rainbow of promise. When we build our lives on these realities, we can shift circumstances and atmospheres from darkness to light and from curse to blessing.

Ashes prove God's fire has burned brightly in our lives. They demonstrate we have sacrificed deeply and personally unto the Lord. They become an ingredient in our lives becoming fertile and fruitful again. And they carry a pleasing aroma up to heaven, where what God inhales becomes an element of the next thing he exhales. To sum it up, the ashes in your life prophesy the rising of your purpose and destiny in the Lord.

INTERNALIZING GOD'S COMFORT

I've brought to you, in every lesson, a heroine or hero of hope, stories of some whose sacrifices are evidence that God's fire has burned within them. I want to inspire you to see your own sacrifices in the same way.

I want you to know that your sacrifice smells really good to God. Yes, I know you might be thinking it stinks to high heaven, and yes, that's exactly what it does. It stinks to the highest heaven. The aroma rises, God breathes it in, and says, *Oh my, what you have gone through, and you've kept your hand on the plow!* Or maybe you didn't keep your hand on the plow, but by God's grace you put it back on, so God says, *That's a sacrifice so well-pleasing to me.*

Take a moment right now to let God's pleasure over your sacrifice sink in. Let it settle over your spirit. Allow that comfort to begin to seep into your heart and mind. You've read the teachings throughout this book, but right now they're getting actualized, like the dots are connecting or the pieces of the puzzle are falling in place. *Yes,* you can say with a sigh of deep relief, *somehow my sacrifice is really pleasing to God.*

If you will grab hold of that hope—that eternal reality—it'll make all the difference. Then you won't be living life looking in the rearview mirror of what has passed you by or what you have passed by, longing to go back there. But you will fix your gaze straight ahead on the future God has for you.

You need to know that God's comfort is there for you, not just for those other people but also for you! He has not forgotten you. He knows you by name. He even takes the time to count and number every hair on your head. I like to playfully think that my lack of hair gives him less to do for me, giving him more time to spend counting yours.

THE BEAUTY REALM OF THE LORD

God wants you to love yourself, but I will tell you, there have been times that I have not liked at all the state that I have been in. A few months ago, I compared a recent picture with a picture of myself ten years ago. I had no idea how bad I looked ten to twelve years ago because I was in the middle of cancer, toxins, radiation, immune therapy, so many drugs and medications, and I was carrying a lot of water weight.

I remember when Heidi Baker looked at me and said, "James, you're doing better, but your color is gray, and you need some help." She referred me to a professional place where I could go to detox. Guess what? God gives beauty for ashes because I look better today than I did ten years ago. I was in the fire. I've been refined by fire. Now I hope I still carry a fire on the inside and that God's fire will radiate through me.

I'm telling you my story, but this is not about me. This is for you because the picture I'm painting is about the master painter. He can take us into his beauty realm and make something beautiful from our ashes.

God gave me an encounter in his beauty realm. I was attending a prophetic conference. Although I was friends with those putting on the conference, it was not a stream I normally minister in, so I kind of held back during the entire conference.

Then the last night, the prophetic worship was so profound that I just couldn't handle it any longer. I went up to the front, stood near some huge speakers, and made one of my lavish statements. I said, "Blast me with everything you got." Well, if God blasted me with everything he has, I would be ashes for sure, but what I got was an interactive encounter with the Lord where he invited me to climb a stairway into heaven, one step at a time.

The stairway would come at times to a plateau. I would stop, and then I would see through the clouds, and as it were, to see another set of stairs. I would climb each new set of stairs I discovered. The higher I went, the more the atmosphere filled with light, majesty, and the brilliant presence of the Lord.

Eventually I came to a platform where I saw the Lord shining in hot, white light. His light was all I could see. This revelation of the beauty of the Lord overwhelmed me. Raptured by his beauty, I started proclaiming over and over again as though I was in the audience of one, "You're beautiful! You are so beautiful!"

I began to sob in the revelation, not out of sorrow, but out of exhilaration. One glance at the beauty of God can make all the sacrifice worth it. David knew this, and tells us so:

> One thing I have asked the Lord, that shall I seek: that I may dwell in the house of the Lord all the days of my life, to behold the beauty of the Lord and to meditate in His temple. For in the day of trouble He will conceal me in His tabernacle; In the secret place of His tent He will hide me; He will lift me up on a rock. And now my head will be lifted

up above my enemies around me, and I will offer in His tent sacrifices with shouts of joy. I will sing, yes, I will sing praises to the Lord. (Psalm 27:4–6 NASB)

Paul also knew this, so he wrote: "But we all, with unveiled face, beholding as in a mirror the glory of the Lord, are being transformed into the same image from glory to glory, just as from the Lord, the Spirit" (2 Corinthians 3:18 NASB). As we gaze upon the beauty of the Lord, we reflect his image. We go from glory to glory, and we become changed into a radiant, shining light. We take on the characteristics of whom or what we behold. What we behold, we become like.

That is a principle the Psalmist gave us. It's a principle that Paul the Apostle gave us. It's a principle that many throughout church history have given us. Madame Jean Dion (Guyon) was one of the people who really opened that up to us. She was a French Christian mystic who wrote the classic book *Experiencing the Inner Depths of the Lord Jesus Christ.* She taught about beholding God through meditation on the Word of God. This meant she would teach people to meditate upon a phrase of the Word until that Word brought you to God himself. That's part of the purpose of the Word of God—to present us to God himself.

THE DIVINE EXCHANGE

This truth that we become what we behold is part of God's strategy in our lives. It is part of the divine exchange. This exchange is no small part of our faith in God. In fact, it is the very center of it, prophesied by Isaiah hundreds of years before Jesus came to fulfill it. I'm going to quote him now, and perhaps this is a well-known passage to you. Or maybe it's brand new to you. Either way, look at it fresh with me:

> For He grew up before Him like a tender shoot, and like a root out of parched ground; He has no stately form or majesty that we should look upon Him, nor appearance that we should be attracted to Him. He was despised and forsaken of men, a man of sorrows and acquainted with grief; and like one from whom men hide their face He was despised, and we did not esteem Him. Surely our griefs He Himself bore, and our sorrows He carried; yet we ourselves esteemed Him stricken, smitten of God, and afflicted. But he was pierced through for our transgressions, He was crushed for our iniquities; the chastening for our well-being fell upon Him, and by His scourging we are healed. (Isaiah 53:2–5 NASB)

Now this takes us from the early years of Jesus all the way to his crucifixion. But it doesn't simply say, "The Messiah will die on a cross." It goes beyond that to detail the divine exchange Jesus offers us.

I would like you to take your hands and put them on your heart right now. I have written some prayer proclamations based on this reality, and I want you to declare them out loud over yourself:

✦ *Jesus took my sorrow, pain, and shame.*

✦ *Jesus, on the cross of Calvary, took the sin of all mankind—generations past, generations present, and generations future.*

+ *It pleased the Father to fling, to put upon him—the spotless Lamb of God—the sin of all mankind.*
+ *Jesus was crushed. He was bruised. He was beaten. He was pierced. He was scourged.*
+ *He did all of this for my well-being, and by his stripes, I am healed.*

This historic exchange happened on the cross of Calvary where Jesus bore our sin and gave us his provision and promise of beauty for ashes. By now we've seen many wonders of this promise, but going back to the theme verse for this chapter, with now the understanding the divine exchange, we read that he gives us more than beauty for ashes. It also says he gives us joy for mourning. And he grants us the garment of praise in divine exchange for the spirit of heaviness. There are three exchanges here, and these are just some of the many exchanges that occurred for us at the cross.

PUTTING ON THE GARMENTS OF PRAISE

God's divine exchange gives us beauty for ashes, joy for our mourning, and a new garment of praise for that which causes us to be heavy. If we are going to receive this exchange, then we also have to make this exchange. We have to cast something off before we can put something new on.

Let's get real. Some of us want to stay clothed in the garments of yesterday. They're familiar. We know them. They bring us comfort. That may be okay for a while, but after a while, those garments become heavy. Even yesterday's great memories become a hindrance to moving forward into your bright tomorrow.

Remember the blind Bartimaeus in Mark 10:46–52. He

couldn't see a thing, but as one sense fails, other senses become heightened. Maybe that's how his knower knew someone was passing by. His feeler felt that there was a person walking in a presence, an anointing. He starts crying out, "Son of David, have mercy on me."

You know what? Eventually he gets Jesus's attention, and you know what he has to do? The gospel writer says, "Throwing aside his cloak, he jumped up and came to Jesus" (Mark 10:50 NASB). He did not take his cloak—his victim mindset—to Jesus. He had to say goodbye to the comfort of yesterday to approach Jesus today to receive the provision for tomorrow.

It is the same for us. Before we can put something new on, we must cast something old off. This takes risk and desperation. I would also say it takes adventure. And it all leads to a moment of standing vulnerable in between the casting off and the putting on. Think about it. What are you once you have cast off what you were wearing? You're naked—vulnerable.

Did you know that in the Old Testament, the priest would take off his garment and stand in front of the tabernacle in public view? He would be stripped and washed and would physically go through a ceremonial bath, naked in public view before he would be robed in the new priestly garments to be able to go into the Holy Place.

Throughout this book, I'm presenting myself vulnerably, standing in between, like the priests of old. We all reach an in-between time, and during this time, we must not compare the past to the future because you do not know what the new garments will look like. Instead, we put on the new garment, resulting in thanksgiving and praise, because now he's not just the God of a second chance; he's the God of the fifty-millionth chance.

TIME TO CHANGE YOUR GARMENTS

Over the years, I've noticed a theme in the Scriptures: the changing of garments. Let's take a moment to consider this natural and spiritual principle. We can start with the example of Joseph, who initially received a multicolored tunic that was supposed to be a symbol of favor and promise. The problem is that his brothers interpreted that garment as something else. In jealousy, they barely avoided murdering him and instead sold him into foreign slavery.

Then from slavery, he descended further when his Egyptian master unjustly cast him into prison. So, from being given a multicolored tunic to wearing prison garments, Joseph was tested. These circumstances also prepared him for the best change of garments, so that when he was lifted from the prison to the palace, he could then wear royal garments in wisdom and humility.

We can continue with the example of Ruth, who, at the beginning of her story in Scripture, was married. I believe she was wonderfully married, but her husband died, she became a widow, and she dressed accordingly in widow's garments. But then the God of another chance came to Ruth when she chose to follow her mother-in-law back to the nation she'd come from—Israel. She became a foreigner and a widow in Israel, but through humility and service, she actually lay at the feet of another. This man, Boaz, took the corner of his garment and placed it over her. She became accepted! In short order, she also became beautified and was able to exchange the garments of a widow for the garments of a bride.

Then we have the example of Lazarus, the friend of Jesus, who died and was wrapped in grave clothes. His body was placed in a tomb, and it lay there for four days. When Jesus appeared on the scene, he called Lazarus forth. John 11:44 describes the scene, "The man who had died came forth, bound hand and foot with wrappings, and his face was wrapped around with a cloth. Jesus said to [his disciples], 'Unbind him and let him go'" (NASB). Once Lazarus was alive again, it would have been inappropriate for him to stay in the grave clothes of his past. They had to rip those off him, and guess what? He would have been vulnerable and naked until someone gave him a new garment to put on.

How about you? What garment do you need to cast off? Are you prepared to be vulnerable in the in-between time? What garments do you need to put on? Remember, he gives us beauty for ashes, joy for mourning, and the garment of praise for the spirit of heaviness. He always offers us the divine exchange.

THE CHALLENGE

I give you a challenge today and give myself the same challenge: Cast off the old. Become vulnerable. Risk being present, so then faith will come alive in your heart all over again. Allow God to take your ashes—that evidence of the fire that has burned within you— and let the pleasing aroma of your sacrifice rise to God. Let it become what he breathes in so that he may breathe out upon you anew.

I want to encourage you in this challenge with Psalm 42:5, "Why are you in despair, O my soul, and why have you become disturbed within me? Hope in God, for I shall again praise Him for the help of His presence" (NASB). His presence is with you always. Let the Holy Spirit wash over your soul and allow praise to rise from the depths within you. Speak to your soul. Tell it to hope again in God!

HEROINE OF HOPE: QUEEN ESTHER

From humble beginnings, Hadassah leaves all she knows to go into a foreign land. Hadassah is Hebrew for "myrtle," an indication that her life and actions were as pleasing as the fragrance of myrtle. Esther, on the other hand, is a Persian name related to "morning star." In Hebrew, it is related to the root word for "hidden," as God's intervention was hidden throughout the entire history-making turn of events.

On the surface, all one sees is a dramatic tale of palace intrigue, but behind the scenes every step is saturated with faith, hope, and sacrificial love. Doubly orphaned as a young girl, Hadassah was raised by her cousin Mordecai, a wise leader of the Jewish people living in exile. After King Ahasuerus dismissed his wife Vashti for insubordination, scouts were sent across the vast Persian Empire to find a replacement. Upon Hadassah's departure for Susa, Mordecai instructed her not to reveal her Jewish identity.

The harem amassed across the kingdom, and the young women were given beauty treatments. Esther's natural beauty and charm caused her to find favor in the eyes of all who saw her. And when her turn came to be presented, the king chose Esther to be his reigning queen.

In a turn of events, Ahasuerus elevated Haman, a notorious anti-Semite, to be his prime minister. Enraged that Mordecai refused to bow to him, Haman asked the king to allow him to have all Jews killed on a single day.

Upon learning of the plot, Mordecai asked Esther to intercede on behalf of her people. Esther agreed to speak to the king, but only if Mordecai and the Jews would fast and pray for three consecutive days. With prayer as her backing, Esther bravely approached Ahasuerus and stood in the gap. Esther's petition for the salvation of the Jewish people was heard. Thus, in an act of intervention, royal decrees were sent out to all provinces declaring protection over the Jewish people.

There are many lessons to be learned from this dear woman, who displayed such humility, bravery, faith, and devotion. But what I want to focus on is the amount of good that came from Queen Esther's reign. She became the reluctant heroine of the biblical Purim story. Taken to the palace of the King of Persia, she was used to expose the plot of evil and prevent the annihilation of all the Jewish people in his extensive empire.

We are each chosen for such a time as this. The transformation of Hadassah into Queen Esther is a dazzling display of how God makes beauty out of ashes. Therefore, I chose Hadassah—Esther—as a heroine of hope.

PRAYER

Heavenly Father, we come to you in the mighty name of Jesus, and we believe that Jesus Christ is the same yesterday, today, and forever. We confess that what he did in the past, he still does today. Help us to take off the garments of heaviness and put on the garments of praise in the way that only you can turn the ash heap of our lives into a masterpiece of beauty, releasing a colorful display of your brilliant presence. Do these marvelous things for the glory of God. Amen and amen.

DISCOVERING HOPE TAKEAWAYS

Chapter 11
Beauty from Ashes

✦ Remember that God gives you beauty from ashes, which reminds you of how his fire has burned in your past. Ultimately, this prophesies the rising of your purpose and destiny in the Lord.

✦ Consider what you need to take off so that you can receive the *new* God wants for you.

✦ God will meet you in the vulnerable in-between time.

✦ Have confidence; God is the God of the fifty-millionth chance

✦ Praise God for the new before you have it. Put on the garment of praise.

CHAPTER 12

AMBASSADORS OF HOPE

To [the Lord's people] God has chosen to make known among the
Gentiles the glorious riches of this mystery, which is Christ in you,
the hope of glory.

COLOSSIANS 1:27 NIV

I wish we lived in a perfect world, but we do not. I have a pastor friend named Ken Roberts whose wife was suddenly killed in a car accident. It was devastating to say the least. Later, after much soul-searching, he remarried and moved from Ohio to Minnesota. He has allowed the Lord to bring wisdom into his life and to convert his personal tragedy into an opportunity to give comfort to others.

While pastoring in Minnesota, a young man named Mike, who had suffered something similar, visited him. Here is what Ken wrote in his blog about their conversation:[8]

> To celebrate their one-year wedding anni-
> versary, Mike and his wife had planned a spe-

---

8   Ken Roberts, "Something Essential for Your Very Survival," posted May 14, 2014 (http://kenlroberts.com).

cial weekend away. Needing to earn some extra money for their upcoming trip, Mike had worked a double shift, returned home, picked up his wife, and headed out on their time away.

As exhaustion overcame excitement, Mike fell asleep at the wheel and slammed into the rear of a semi-truck, killing his wife and unborn child. He now sat across the table from me at a local diner.

At first our conversation was awkward, but ... after a few hours, I gently offered him some advice out of my own experience and brokenness ... [Ken shared how a seasoned pastor named C. Neil Strait had put it:] "Take from a man his wealth, and you hinder him; take from him his purpose, and you slow him down. But take from man his hope, and you stop him. He can go on without wealth, and even without purpose, for a while. But he will not go on without hope."

Ken went on to share a quote from a former P.O.W. named David Jacobsen, who was beaten and tortured for over seventeen months. After he was released and returned to the United States, a reporter asked him, "Mr. Jacobsen, what kept you alive during the many months of extreme cruelty and the daily uncertainty of whether you would live or die?" and David's immediate response was this: "Hope was the nourishment for my survival."

Again and again you hear it: _Hope_ is the key for endurance. And Ken is modeling what it means to be an ambassador of hope.

Having discovered its primary importance, he is adding his testimony to that of so many others.

I CAN DO ALL THINGS THROUGH CHRIST

I shared earlier that after Michal Ann died, I started to keep a personal journal so I would have a place to pour out my raw emotions and to start to feel my way toward solid ground again. After a year, I felt that the Holy Spirit wanted me to close that journal and start a new one. I thought I might name that one, "The Journal of a Hopeful Man," but soon I realized I wasn't there yet. I could not live a lie, so I altered the title to "The Journey of an Adventurous Man," and that felt right. I used that volume to write down my thoughts and discoveries as well as I could for the past few years. Then finally, I felt I could start a journal called "The Journal of a Hopeful Man," which is still the one I write in from time to time today.

During those years, I still had to preach and teach, and it was almost impossible to give of myself. I felt so dead inside. I kept combing through Scripture looking for life. And one of the places I found the most hope for myself personally was in Paul's epistle to the Philippians.

You will remember that during that first year after my wife's death, cancer came back with a vengeance, and it nearly took me out. So as I was fighting not only for hope but also for my very survival, Philippians 4:13 became my friend: "I can do all things through Christ who strengthens me" (NKJV). *I can do this. I might feel alone, but God is with me.*

Another verse from Philippians that I had known well for years was driven home for me in a new way: "For I am confident of this very thing, that He who began a good work in you will perfect it until the day of Christ Jesus" (Philippians 1:6 NASB). In my debilitated state, this meant the world to me—God's work in my life was not up to me. I could depend upon his strength. I could be sure of the fact that he was not going to give up on me. *It's not up to me. I may get discouraged and confused, but God does not. He will carry me, and we will cross the finish line together.*

Then for more than a whole year, this verse that Paul wrote to the Philippians sustained me:

> I have great joy in the Lord because now at last you have again expressed your concern for me. (Now I know you were concerned before but had no opportunity to do anything.) I am not saying this because I am in need, for *I have learned to be content in any circumstance.* (Philippians 4:10–11 NET, emphasis added)

"I have learned to be content in any circumstance." Those few words brought me so much of God's grace. They brought me sanity. They showed me God's mercy in the midst of frailty.

Paul's choice of words encouraged me because he did not say, "I was always perfectly content" or "I am comfortable" or even "I am content." He said, "I have *learned* to be content in any circumstance." I knew that Paul was buffeted by endless difficulties, many of them life-threatening. He was imprisoned, beaten, stoned, quarreled with, shipwrecked. He had a feisty personality, which says to me that he was not naturally contented. But he learned. And if Paul could learn how to be content with endless hits, so can I. God will teach me too. *God is in touch with me. He knows how hard it is. I am one of his own, like Paul, and I can learn to be content too. If that means as a widower, then as a widower. If that means as married, then that means as married.* My goal was to learn to become content.

A fourth and very special verse from Philippians spoke to my practical needs: "And my God will supply all your needs according to His riches in glory in Christ Jesus" (Philippians 4:19 NASB). I had a lot of needs. From earlier in this book, you will remember that I was facing three hundred thousand dollars of medical debt and that I had lost over half of my financial supporters. It was an impossible situation. But with unexpected help, financial counseling, debt consolidation, and sheer diligence, I have now paid off all of it.

During that same period, my two sons and two daughters all got married—and God provided an amazing spouse for each of them. Now I have been cancer-free for over nine years, and my oncologist has released me from his care; I just go back for yearly checkups. I am healed, and I can declare that cancer is never, ever coming back. I will never get my Michal Ann back, but I know that as I learn to be content as a single widower, God will take care of me one way or the other. *God, you have supplied all my needs, and I know you will continue to supply them. I can trust you with every detail of my life.*

As I consider my *Journal of a Hopeful Man,* I want more than ever to become a man of hope. I want to be able to share the good news that our God is a God of hope, our hope-builder. I want to be an ambassador of hope for the sake of others, repeating the powerful truths that he has taught me: God is good all the time. All things work together for good. Something good is about to happen.

I want to participate with God in bringing hope solutions to gritty, real-life problems. This might not always be a one-on-one ambassadorship; it might reach whole cities or even nations. Not long ago I traveled to minister in the city of Detroit, which looked like a war zone, and God spoke to me in dreams twice in the same night. In the first, he said, *Where there's desolation, there will be restoration.* In the second, he said, *Every place where there is devastation, there will be transformation.* How will God's restoration and transformation look? Better than the original, most likely. Ambassadors of hope learn to think big, as God does.

ABOUNDING HOPE

Hope is such a little word, but it holds tremendous power. Romans 15:13 announces that faith and the power of the Holy Spirit combined enable us to *abound* in hope. Hope makes us comeback kids, equipped for anything.

Where do we look for hope? We start with the written Word: "For everything that was written in the past was written to teach us, so that through the endurance taught in the Scriptures and the encouragement they provide we might have hope" (Romans 15:4 NIV). As we search through both the Old Testament and the New, one "hope nugget" leads to the next.

For example, I read the words of Lamentations: "This I recall to my mind, therefore I have hope. Through the Lord's mercies we are not consumed, because His compassions fail not. They are new every morning; great is Your faithfulness" (Lamentations 3:21–23 NKJV). But when I decided to put those words into practice, I did not know how to overcome my inertia; I found that I was unable to appreciate God's provisions anew every morning. What could I do about that? I could talk to myself. I could say, *Why, my soul, are you downcast? Why so disturbed within me? Put your hope in God, for I will yet praise him, my Savior and my God* (Psalm 43:5 NIV). "Put your hope in God"—that is an imperative statement, actually, a command to my soul. I needed to exercise myself a little. I needed to *put* my hope in God and to *put* on my helmet of hope (remember 1 Thessalonians 5:8 from chapter 3), which will protect my thoughts and my perceptions and shield my mind from negative hope-destroyers.

Once we come to Christ Jesus, we get to know hope in person, because hope is a person: "Christ in you, the hope of glory" (Colossians 1:27 NIV). Before we knew Christ, we were "without hope and without God" (Ephesians 2:12 NIV), walking in the dark. Now we can dispel darkness wherever we find ourselves, overflowing with gratitude to God and abounding in the hope he has supplied for us. We are able to look beyond our present circumstances because we hold the ultimate hope, what Paul calls "the blessed hope [of] the appearing of the glory of our great God and Savior, Jesus Christ" (Titus 2:13 NIV).

SHARING HOPE

One of the ways I try to encourage others is in the form of sharing encouraging quotes via social media. Each morning, before I get out of bed, I start my day by sharing a quote that will inspire others to hang onto the hope that keeps us on track with God. Below are ten quotes I've found on the internet and have shared on Instagram or Facebook. If you follow me, you may have seen some of these before:

+ Just because you don't see a way doesn't mean God doesn't have one.
+ If you can't fly—run. If you can't run—walk. If you can't walk—crawl. But by all means keep moving!

✦ You can't start the next chapter of your life if you keep re-reading the last one.

✦ God loves you even when you can't find the strength to love yourself.

✦ God says, *Prepare yourself. I'm about to take you to another level in your life.*

✦ The greatest test of faith is when you don't get what you want, but still you are able to say, *Thank you, Lord.*

✦ Sorrow looks back. Worry looks around. Faith looks up!

✦ Blessings are headed your way!

✦ In the end, we only regret the chances we didn't take.

✦ Never mistake the silence of God for the absence of God. Don't lose trust because you can't understand. He's always working.

This is just one small way I'm trying to share hope with others, encouraging them to find hope and rediscover life after tragedy. What are some ways you can be an ambassador of hope?

I cling to the life lessons I have been learning. Trials and difficulties have not ended for me. I have not even begun to tell you about a failed back surgery that resulted in damage to my sciatic nerves. I have lived in excruciating pain for over five years. But God! And guess what? Even our God of hope is using all of this as well. I am on another great learning curve, including the subjects of physical therapy, nutrition, essential oils, and so much more. I will not quit! I am even going to be featured in a celebrity art gallery show in a distinct, black and white photo with a short testimony called "But God!" Huh!

Maybe I am becoming a Renaissance man after all. I am still taking lessons in my new class of discovering hope for your life. And

I am being healed from the inside out. Every morning, I declare to myself, *Miracles are mine. Miracles are coming to me, and miracles are flowing through me. I am one day closer to my miracle.*

HEROES OF HOPE: NOW IT'S YOUR TURN

In the previous eleven chapters, I have profiled a diversity of people from both past and present. They represent many different walks of life. Now it is your turn to be the next hero or heroine of hope. I am nominating *you* as a candidate for the latest ambassadorship of hope, and I am basing my nomination on the following passage: "So we are Christ's ambassadors; God is making his appeal through us. We speak for Christ when we plead, 'Come back to God!'" (2 Corinthians 5:20 NLT).

An ambassador goes to his or her appointed place, having been vested with authority to represent one nation to another. In this case, you will be representing the kingdom of God to the world at large. Just as the red carpet may be rolled out for an earthly ambassador, so you step out onto the red blood of Jesus, ready to make an impact.

The world needs you. Hope solutions are in short supply. And one of the best ways to find hope is to give hope away. The world needs vibrant believers who have won their way through monumental obstacles and who can show the way of hope. Hope ambassadors know hope inside out. They breathe hope, live hope, exhibit hope, and light up their sphere of influence with hope. By the grace that God supplies, I commission you to be an ambassador of hope!

So how are you going to give hope away? Ask God to open your eyes to the many opportunities around you and then see how you can comfort those who are in any affliction with the same comfort you have received from God (see 2 Corinthians 1:3-4).

I also invite you to partner with me in my new Mentoring with James program. I am inviting others to go on the journey with me to grow in wisdom and stature and favor with God and man through prayer, the prophetic, and the presence of God. I want to give transferrable concepts to help you discover hope for your journey. (Visit mentoringwithjames.com/GEM for more information or to be a new participant.)

Out of the ash heap of my own life experience, my Creator is fashioning something beautiful. And guess what? He is an equal opportunity God waiting to do something for you beyond your imagination. I am out here covering my part of the territory. How about you? Will you volunteer to be the next ambassador of hope?

PRAYER

Father God, by your grace I choose to
take my place in the theater of life. I want to
play my role in your grand drama with its many
acts. I am grateful and delighted to be given
another opportunity to learn about you and to
sit at your feet. I believe and declare that you
are good all the time and your mercies endure
forever. I receive my commissioning as an
ambassador of hope. Fill me with your Holy
Spirit and with your heavenly perspective so
that I will always represent you well. Through
Jesus, your Son. Amen.

DISCOVERING HOPE TAKEAWAYS

Chapter 12
Ambassadors of Hope

✦ Now that you have hope, you know that you can do all things through Christ Jesus, who strengthens you. You are sure that God will supply all your needs (read Philippians 4:13, 19).

✦ As you experience God's care, you will want to share with others what God has taught you:

- He is the source of all true hope, all true wisdom, all true strength.
- He brings solutions to real problems.
- God is good all the time, and he works all things together for good—for you!

About the Author

Dr. James W. Goll is the founder of God Encounters Ministries. He is an international bestselling author, a certified Life Language Coach, and a recording artist who has also ministered in more than fifty nations. James is also the founder of GOLL Ideation LLC, where creativity, consulting, and leadership training come together.

James was married to Michal Ann for thirty-two years before her graduation to heaven in the fall of 2008. He has four adult married children and a growing number of grandchildren. James continues to make his home in Franklin, Tennessee.

For More Information

James W. Goll
God Encounters Ministries
P.O. Box 1653
Franklin, TN 37065
Phone: 1-877-200-1604

Websites:

www.godencounters.com
mentoringwithjames.com/GEM

E-mail:

info@godencounters.com
invitejames@godencounters.com

Social Media Tools:

Facebook, Instagram, Twitter, GEM Media, God Encounters
Today Podcast, XPMedia, Kingdom Flame, YouTube, Vimeo,
Charisma Blog, and iTunes

OTHER BOOKS BY JAMES W. GOLL

Adventures in the Prophetic
A Radical Faith
Angelic Encounters
Deliverance from Darkness
Dream Language
Empowered Prayer
Empowered Women
Fearless and Free
God Encounters Today
Hearing God's Voice Today
Living a Supernatural Life
Passionate Pursuit
Prayer Storm
Praying for Israel's Destiny
Praying with God's Heart
Releasing Spiritual Gifts Today
The Call to the Elijah Revolution
The Coming Israel Awakening
The Discerner
The Lifestyle of a Prophet
The Lifestyle of a Watchman
The Lost Art of Intercession
The Lost Art of Practicing His Presence
The Lost Art of Pure Worship
The Prophet
The Seer
What Love Looks Like
Strike the Mark

Numerous study guides are also available and entire curriculum kits including corresponding CD and MP3 albums and/or DVD and MP4 messages.